Alive & Well

The simplicity behind getting your customers' loyalty... and keeping it.

by

Lalo Duron, PhD

With a foreword by

José Antonio Fernández Carbajal

Copyright © 2019 by Lalo Duron
Foreword copyright © 2019 by José Antonio Fernández Carbajal

All rights reserved.

Edited by Anapaula Duron

First Edition

To Ramón García.

– Old man, reading from *Report to Greco*:

Son, what do you think of this?: "Look – if you can– at fear right in the eye. Fear will be afraid and leave."

– Kid: *Grandpa, Fear is invisible.*

Acapulco. 1969.

This is a work of fiction. Names, characters, businesses, places, events, locales, and incidents are either the products of the author's imagination or used in a fictitious manner. Any resemblance to actual persons, living or dead, or actual events is purely coincidental.

TABLE OF CONTENTS

Foreword	15
Customer loyalty is dead… or is it not?	18
It's not what you know; it's what you can do.	26
Eureka!	34
Trouble starts where and when you least expect it.	47
The story of three dreamers who wanted glory back.	54
Think and do ain't the same thing.	61
Things you'll see, dear Sancho.	75
Yes, and…	84
And they rode off into the sunset.	92
If I tell you, it wouldn't be magic.	95
The secret to great Mole is to know how.	116
Who's gonna do it? How?	128
Enough talk. Now, let's do it.	153
On the road again.	164
Ready, set, swim!	174

Foreword

If we combine a disciplined team's performance with the results provided by our customer's loyalty –and a bit of good luck– we get the most desired results regarding a company's expected performance: Excellence. As an example; FEMSA has grown to become a company valued with a net worth of $30 billion dollars and approximately 300,000 employees. It is known to be the biggest beverage company in Latin America and owns the largest worldwide and most profitable Coca Cola franchise bottler-retailer in the region. I have had the very good fortune of running this company, first as its CEO –from 1995 to 2014– and currently as Executive Chairman of the board of directors.

Through time, I have learned a thing or two about a company's success; I really think that it relies on achieving customer loyalty to become a thriving business. I'm convinced that there is no better way to obtain this than by encouraging consistent team work and trust between team players in order to successfully achieve all the company's goals.

You might think that specialists have already written everything there is to know about the most precious secrets on what services and brands' customers expect. Let me tell you something: they haven't. I am a true believer that one should never stop learning and trying to deeply understand what customers are expecting when they acquire a service or a product. It is true that we are facing times of high global competitiveness, which are also combined with high-end technology that has provided all our customers with easy-to-reach information, mainly through portable electronic devices. These digital transformations create an urge within companies-to change the way we think and act through the evolution of new generations.

Throughout the years I have personally experienced the transformation of business models that are based on strategic premises; these strategies clearly outline what we believe to be the right definition of the mission, vision and values. We usually experience changes through restructures that force us to take a couple of steps back and rethink our strategy in order to understand and favor our customers' preferences on our products and services. I think it is precisely why the concern about these issues makes a book like "Alive & Well" a helpful guide for we business people to feed and increase our knowledge, in order to understand and analyze customer's habits and consumption.

Dr. Lalo Duron explains, in a very entertaining, easy to read, and straightforward analysis –which compiles exemplary fresh and up to date information– that allows us to ponder the importance on what it is that keeps breaking paradigms along the line of some questions like: "Who is in charge here? The customers are. Why? Because we live on the money they give us. That gives them all the power".

This book brilliantly describes how concepts like the three-dimensional loyalty outline –in which Lalo details what is it that companies do for their Customers – impact on the purchase of the company's products or services. He also questions if companies are really attending their customers' needs; it got me thinking that, in addition to the companies' urge to keep their customers' interests at hand, they also need to consider general business ecosystems, for it is extremely important to have a sustainable operational business model that would keep companies going while strengthening their customers interest on the products or services they provide. I solely think that social interaction – which can result in a true lasting interaction of the customer-provided loyalty– would ultimately show that the company has a genuine interest in their customers' and also the planet's needs.

In the future, companies must prioritize both economic and social impact in order to create a complete sustainable business for the long run. We must see companies as enablers of social mobility and financial inclusion and not only leave all the responsibility of those actions to governmental policies. It is useless if companies have a correct balance between economic and social value if they lose sight of the continuous, emerging demands from new consumers such as the up and coming techy generations like millennials and generation Z.

All of the above just leads me to emphasize that in addition of being at the forefront of innovation while adapting to new trends and technologies –readers will enjoy the trip Lalo invites us to take on our way to the pursuit of Customer loyalty.

José Antonio Fernández Carbajal
Executive Chairman of the Board of Directors, FEMSA

Customer loyalty is dead... or is it not?

> *I see people purchasing the latest iPhone and Galaxys every year; is customer loyalty really dead?*

Treat customers according to their value and needs, and they will be loyal to you. I read Enterprise One to One back in 1995, and fell in love with its proposal.

Treat different customers differently became one of my favorite business mantras. Value your customers; identify what they need, and treat them accordingly.

Genius, right?

Time passed and I started seeing how customer loyalty was the holy grail of marketing and business people… yet only a few companies tried to do something about it, beyond reward programs:- If you use my service, I will give you something in return –points, miles, a seal, anything usable as a token will do. If you stop using them, too bad. You will get nothing from me and I will forget you.

Companies such as airlines, banks, or hotels, started using this strategy of rewarding repeated usage by frequent customers, while forgetting those who left … and it took its toll. As years went by, companies began losing customers without having a clear idea as to why Customers were leaving, opening a hole in revenues and profits, and no one was capable of diagnosing what was happening.

So, somebody came with a proper answer; an answer the business community was expecting for years; the scapegoat for the marketing, service and management professionals:

CUSTOMER LOYALTY IS DEAD.

It was a thesis that explained quite well the things companies were going through. During the dawn of 21st century, it was easier to blame the customer than admitting something was done wrong and it was not on the customers' side.

Some software companies came up with a solution which made lots of sense: Let's make our customers the right offer, thru the right channel, at the right time. It meant putting into action what Peppers and Rogers proposed back in '94, selecting target customers according to their value and needs, presenting offerings that match their consumption patterns and predicted needs, sending the resulting offer using a channel fit to the customer's preference, at the time when it could be more effective.

It made lots of sense, but it didn't work. Some companies tried it and found it required lots of data –which wasn't perceived as a good source for customer understanding at the time– and long, complicated software implementation projects which were prone to failure by not using hard metrics to measure their success.

It was the momentum the myth required.

CUSTOMER LOYALTY HAS TO BE DEAD. WE TRIED CRM AND NOTHING HAPPENED.

Instead of inspiring any action, the myth became a pillar for resistance. Managers from many companies, lines of business, and industries, started convincing themselves about customer disloyalty, fueled by how easy change had become, and price wars.

Then came the final cut: millennials. These guys born at the end of 20th century (who'd be of age at the turn of the century) had behavioral and attitudinal characteristics that made them very different from the previous generations, X, Baby Boomers and Silent.

Millennials were just what the management community needed to turn the myth into a business truth. Loyalty is dead, so our revenues are not growing. Loyalty is dead, so our markets shrink. Loyalty is dead so our customer turnover is way higher than expected. Loyalty is dead, so we are condemned.

WHAT? REALLY?

Even when managers' role is to lead companies to success, they are regular Joes who also make mistakes and fail, and when it happens they look for an excuse… just another name for "cause". The bigger the failure, and the harder to find the cause, the bigger the excuse. The case of Customer Loyalty –aka Brand Loyalty or Loyalty– was a lost one: Since we can not control our customer base deterioration, we explain it in terms of external variables, and the easiest one is this:

CUSTOMERS' LOYALTY TO A BRAND IS DEAD, SO WE HAVE NOTHING TO DO BUT TO FASTEN OUR SEAT BELTS.

It is most likely that you and I haven't met, and if you'd known me from between 1995 and 2010, you'd surely know about my personal view regarding customer loyalty. I was convinced customer loyalty was well and alive, and it could be measured in a very simple manner, related to how often and how much your customer purchased from you. From there, you could calculate customer value and focus on those with the highest value –I even wrote articles and gave speeches on the subject.

I was so convinced about it, I even designed a valuation model to differentiate customers based on their purchasing patterns, the amount spent, the strategic value and the probability of the customer to keep purchasing from the company. I even published it in a well-known trade magazine, and helped my clients adopt it.

My argument was some customers were more valuable than others, based on their behavior, and it was all I needed as conceptual support for my loyalty model. A loyal customer is one that purchases with the most frequency, spending the most money on our brand. And I felt quite comfortable with it, defended it on different forums, and made it a part of my day-to-day practice.

When I talked to students or audiences, or wrote something, my opinion on loyalty was based on money spent and frequency. It was based on consumer behavior.

I was indeed a promoter of RFM, the good ol' model for measuring customer loyalty based on recency, frequency and monetary value. A simple, yet effective manner to define customers' value from three variables: how long had it been from their last purchase, how often they purchase from us, and how much they had spent on us during their lifetime. Simple and effective.

Then, around 2008, something happened that changed my perception forever... and for good.

I had an MBA teacher who later became my friend; Luis Herrera invited me to be his co-teacher at EGADE Business School, Tec de Monterrey's graduate business school. He asked me to deliver the session where he discussed customer loyalty, with a very nice approach: Creating long term relationships with customers.

It was my personal tipping point. I started having long conversations with Luis –by then, Dr. Herrera, as I found out later– and some discussions aimed to improve my subject. We spent hours talking about Marketing One to One, CRM and reward programs, and their effects on customer loyalty. It was a term we rarely discussed, and there we were, talking about the tools to measure it and make it useful for the brands; it then became one of our regular topics

UNTIL...

Out of the blue, Luis asked me how I defined customer loyalty. I gave him my answer. He asked me to define the model I used to define who a loyal customer was, and I did. Then, one of the most memorable, long and useful discussions of my life started.

"Why do you measure loyalty on the behavioral side, leaving out customer's attitude?", he asked. I defended myself saying that attitude was not needed, since all that mattered to measure loyalty was based on transactional variables; Luis, being the intelligent and good friend that he was, insisted.

The discussion lasted several days, if not weeks, forcing me to revisit original concepts, readings and articles until I found something, an eye opener. Back in '94, the same year Peppers and Rogers published one of their books, two researchers, Alan Dick and Kunal Basu defined customer loyalty as a combination of two variables: attitude and behavior. Customers who spent with a high frequency and no positive attitude towards the brand, were known as spurious loyals. Those who bought as often as they can, with a positive attitude, were the true loyals.

FOUND IT!

My original definition of customer loyalty was indeed in conflict with attitude, and I was missing the difference between true and spurious loyalty. An important difference, it turned out, since a relationship with a true loyal is based on a positive relationship, while a spurious one is there for some benefits that may be replaced in a snap when things get a little rough –just as in any human relationship, attitude has a lot to do to keep them healthy and long-lasting.

It was almost a mystical finding, and I intended to make the most of it. Loyalty was not only a function of how often and how much customers spent; it was also related to how good a relationship with the brand they had.

Then, I started my doctoral studies. Since I was in charge of the marketing and sales area of a direct marketing company –and an active member of our professional association for many years then– I designed my research to identify the effects of commercial communications on customers' loyalty to a brand.

It was a logical subject. Besides the new loyalty model, I had just proposed, I was also convinced that brand loyalty was achieved thru direct, frequent and differentiated communications, and all of them had a positive correlation: the better, more frequent and differentiated the communications were, the better loyalty was.

I had a very clear objective on mind. I would discover the real relationship of marketing communications on customers' loyalty to a brand, to further confirm or deny the current perception or causes and effect about customer loyalty.

The toughest part of my journey was just beginning.

TAKE AWAYS

Customer loyalty is not dead; disloyalty is a great excuse for lousy execution when it comes to satisfy customers.

Models such as RFM are good proxies for customer loyalty, even when they focus on the transactional part.

Customer Loyalty has two elements: attitude and behavior. Your job is to go for both and stimulate them.

Even if you are convinced about something, discuss it, be critical about it. It may reinforce your beliefs, or it can change them: Both cases are good.

It's not what you know; it's what you can do.

— Who's in charge here?
— The customers are.
— Why?
— Because we live from the money they give us.
That gives them all the power.

I was in the phase where I had to gather data to make further analysis, get conclusions to present in my thesis... and it wasn't working at all. I had selected a qualitative approach to discover how people saw loyalty and communications, and their perception about how they were related. So, I decided I would use focus groups, together with some interviews with industry specialists.

The interviews were easy; specialists were eager to express and discuss their points of view, their experiences and knowledge, and the interviews turned out to be quite straight forward.

Regular people, they were tough cookies. If you are familiar with focus groups, you know how complicated it may be to get people to attend one, and once they are there, how easy it is for them to get them deviated from the objective by a spontaneous leader, a lousy facilitator, or environmental distractions. I passed through all of those cases. It was a dead-end situation until I got the best advice I could get: "Do Tupperware-like parties. Ask friends who have enough weight on their social network, to invite some of their own friends for an evening of coffee and cookies".

It worked better than expected. I had the opportunity to be in conversations with people who were consumers – loyal or not– from many service companies, either airlines, banks, phone companies, and open to discuss how those companies were doing on achieving their loyalty.

A regular focus group session is supposed to last less than an hour, to keep the attendees focused and interested. Mine were much longer than that. From one and a half hours to three hours, those coffee sessions were great sources of insights and understanding, the biggest of them being: "So they treat me as a queen".

So, they treat me as a queen.

It was a shocker. Before those sessions, I was convinced that marketing communications were the main reason for customer loyalty, and that insight sent the concept crumbling down.

Not that I felt any sorrow, no. I felt energized. There was another way to put things together, other variables to work with to achieve customer loyalty… and I was on the path to discover them.

As a professional practitioner, my day-to-day life was that of a marketing engineer. As founding partner and planning principal, I had to deal with our own customers' requests, and deliver the value they expected. It meant I had too little time for putting together what I had found – pages and pages of transcripts and notes were yet to be analyzed to get any meaning from them.

Life is full of mystery and happy coincidences, and mine is not the exception. I got an invitation from Schulich School of Business to spend a summer there as a researcher, a great excuse so I could finish sketching my thesis' model.

I did. I spent the summer in Toronto and lived a real Eureka moment. I understood Archimedes' joy when he realized his principle just from immersing in a tub. I was in a garden, on a sunny day, under a blue sky spotted with white cotton-like clouds. Just like in the classical biographies, the idea of a model came up like an explosion, like an epiphany, and it explained it all.

All the results and research categories I put together, made sense when I grouped them into three major groups:

First, I had clear evidence that people expect to receive what they were promised; not more, not less, just what they were offered, what they pay for. There's this catchy phrase that goes "Exceed your customer's expectations". Come on! First of all, you have to guarantee meeting their expectations, so they are satisfied with the relationship. Passengers expect the flight to leave and arrive on time, and to get there at the same time as their luggage. Exceed their expectations? No; they basically want you to meet their expectations and needs: get to their destination, together with all the checked suitcases, all of them safe and sound. If you want to exceed them, it's kind of optional.

Second, and it was some sort of relief, the brand and its customers need to be communicated. Bi-directional channels are great to send and receive messages about how the relationship is going, what new offers the brand has, what the customers are getting or feeling. Communication is something the customers expect and are grateful for.

Nowadays, communications between a brand and its consumers are easier, faster and swifter than ever. A mass media communications campaign may be the one with the longest times to create, launch and modify... yet it works quite well. On the other hand, digital and direct communications are a great situation; they can be prepared, launched, measured and, if needed, corrected, in a very short time. Social Media is a facilitator for direct, non-mediated communications between a brand and its market.

So, communications held their position as an element of loyalty, yet not the only one: keep fluent, two way communications with your market, and let them be your ears to get the buzz from the bees, so you can trigger the right reaction when you need to.

And third. Third one's a winner, they say.

Remember that phrase "so they treat me like a queen"? Well, it was a call for getting great service, for being treated on such a manner that customers feel they are getting much more attention, much more service than they had expected when asking for the brand's services or products.

What's the difference between a memorable flight with *United* and *Emirates*? It is not the flight itself, not the duration nor the route the pilots take… it is service, the way crews treat the passengers and make them feel well or ill treated –a real deal breaker when things go bad (right, United?).

Service became the third element, complementing the first two. The three of them, together, were able to include all the variables my initial research had found –with a bonus: They were less than four, which is the maximum number of variables a regular person can handle.

A simple statement could express the model: Loyalty is a result of the offer, the communications, and the service the customer gets.

Simple, yet comprehensive. The model explained quite well how companies such as Starbucks, Telcel, or American Express were shaping their relationships with their customers to expect a better, lasting relationship.

Some context: I am an industrial engineer and, as such, I devised (with some help of a student) a vectorial model which represented the loyalty function. It worked as a clockwork, but it was difficult for regular Joe to understand and manage.

My new research objective then became to create a management model to help managers implement and manage loyalty to the brand. With this model, it was easier for me to define how to do it, and which profiles were needed to accomplish the task.

Remember I started this book mentioning the business legend about customer loyalty being dead? Data showing decline on sales, customer churn, and other transactional elements are used to support this claim. So, how come the legend doesn't tell a thing about customer satisfaction, nor reasons why customers leave, or how the fault may not be charged upon the brands –but on the customers?

Because we are sapiens. More than just humans, we are homo sapiens and, as Harari put it, when we cannot control the environment we feel uncomfortable. If we have no way to control our customers, it is easier to blame one of the mean three, famine, war or illness.

Marketing is war, ergo everybody is out there trying to take our customers away from us; competitors are pathogenic agents, who get our systems ill and cause our customer base to die; or the market has switched habits, which has created migrations where we are left with no customers to forage. One of them **has** to be the answer for customer loss; not that we are to blame nor guilty of anything.

So?

Harari, on *Homo Deus*, says something quite simple. We want to reach divinity. To live forever and reach happiness are goals which the sapiens species has pursued for ages and now seem closer to hand than ever... so I ask: Are we looking for divinity just for our lives, or for our creations too?

Because our brands, our companies and organizations are, somehow, our creatures, it is our responsibility to bring joy and eternal life to them. Yet, blaming the environment, the competition and the customers for our faults seems to be the right thing to do. Is it?

No, it is not, and we will discuss in further detail how are we in the position to be more than mere victims and get to the role of creators, entities in charge of making our organizations' environment safer, healthier and wealthier for our organizations... without putting their lives in jeopardy.

Let me tell you a story on how I did it. It will take a few chapters, and afterwards I will give you a tour of the final formula to get your customers to keep purchasing from you, with a positive attitude toward your brand, despite your competition's efforts to take them away.

Are you ready? Let me tell you a story about my work with Graham.

TAKE AWAYS.

Treat me like a queen.

It's a war out there; don't blame your customer nor competition for customer loss. Blame your self.

Loyalty is a result of the offer, the communications, and the service the customer gets.

Eureka!

There's no emotion like the one that comes from discovery, from invention.

Having lunch at the library's garden, after several months trying to shape my vision on how to get and manage customers' loyalty to a brand, I got struck by inspiration. Eureka!, I thought, sitting there with a sandwich, some orange juice, and nobody to share it with.

For years, I had listened to customers, professionals and peers saying, "loyalty is dead", to such an extent that I started to believe it. I knew marketing communications were not enough, business intelligence was not enough, direct marketing was not enough, sales forces were not enough, and that made me wonder: What's enough? How can a brand earn customer loyalty? Is it manageable?

Inspiration struck. A Canadian summer day gave me the idea. It was not a matter of one thing or the other; it was one thing, and the other, and the other. Three things together, working in unison, were responsible to achieve and maintain a customer's loyalty to a service brand: bidirectional communications, fulfilling the offer, and service. The way they were connected had eluded me for months, and now their relationship was clear: they work at unison, impacting different aspects of the customer-vendor relationship, and, best of all, they are manageable.

Eureka!, I said again. I was happy, happier than I could've imagined, even though I was not Aristotle and hadn't discovered a world changing principle. I had devised a way to change the business world, managing customer loyalty for the good of both the customers and service brands.

As the expression, I begin this chapter with goes, there's no emotion like that coming from discovering things, from inventing them. The joy of putting different elements together and discover how they will change things in unexpected ways is equal to none. I was thrilled. I made a thought experiment just like giants such as Einstein and Hawking did. Thinking hard feels great!

What was all my fuzz about? Simple. It all started a couple of years before...

After a conversation with Universidad de Celaya's dean, I accepted the challenge to study a doctorate, and stated an initial thesis: "Customers' loyalty to a brand depends on direct marketing communications from the brand to them". I believed it and was eager to demonstrate there was causality between direct communications and brand loyalty, so my research was orchestrated on such a manner that it could be demonstrated.

Then, something unexpected happened. After conducting in-depth interviews and focus groups with consumers from service brands, such as airlines, phone companies, banks, I found no direct causation between communications and loyalty. It was more of a mix, where I saw many factors influencing loyalty.

And the unexpected? It came via an invitation from Schulich, York University's school of business, to spend one summer over there, researching, thinking and writing my thesis. I accepted.

Going to Toronto was a great decision. Schulich's library and gardens were the place to be if you had something to think about. My sister lived there, in a beautiful house, and the summer internship turned into a great working holiday, when I had the chance to do the research and thinking I needed, while spending a great time with my little sister, whose company I hadn't enjoyed for many years.

As all of you know, magic works in beautiful ways, and this was not to be an exception. One of those summer days, when I was having lunch on the library's garden, under a blue sky full of cotton white clouds, I saw it. Communications, offer, and customer orientation were independent and it is possible to work on one element without affecting the others. They were independent variables, so the answer to my search was...

A three dimensional model!

No, loyalty was not the result of direct communications. It was the mix of three elements, all of them working together, independent from the other two.

First, what the customer bought from the company, the offer, is fundamental. People expect something when they hire a service company, and getting it is a reason to keep purchasing from it.

Then, what the customer and the company tell to each other, the communications, are important too. A brand has to keep telling the customer what is going on, what will happen, what new things are available for the customer to get; and the brand must listen to its customers, to be aware about what's going on with them, what they expect, what they think, what they are getting, and how satisfied they are.

Last, what the company does for the customers, how it treats them, what they get besides the basic service they purchased, the attention the company pays to their needs, and how does it fulfill them, based on factors beyond "the customer is always right".

Those three came together, and worked fine both alone and combined. They were independent variables. My inner engineer was ecstatic. Yes, it was an epiphany, my eureka moment, and I reacted with real joy. Wouldn't you?

From then, everything got feverish; one thing was to define my model as a three elements thing; defining it, making it understandable and, above all, implementable was a deeper, was a more complicated thing. I was proud of defining myself as a marketing engineer, so I approached the task with a mix of marketing and engineering, to get a result I liked very much: The COS Model, which made Brand Loyalty a result of three independent variables, Offer, Communications and Service.

Wow! I had it! The COS Model.

A three-dimensional model meant it was simpler to define loyalty, focusing on issues relevant to motivating customers to prefer a brand above its competitors, even against the efforts they made to gain their favor. Yep, this was a good definition of loyalty, it only needed some refining to make it usable for managers and executives looking for the whole enchilada: brand loyalty.

Now, there was an issue: How to draw the model? Was it a sphere? A cube? A rectangular prism? I was having a complicated time trying to find the best way to express the model, with a graphic, a figure, even a sphere capable of transmitting its characteristics on a glimpse. I just couldn't do it and I was beginning to feel my hands tied, unable to transmit what I had thought on that sunny day.

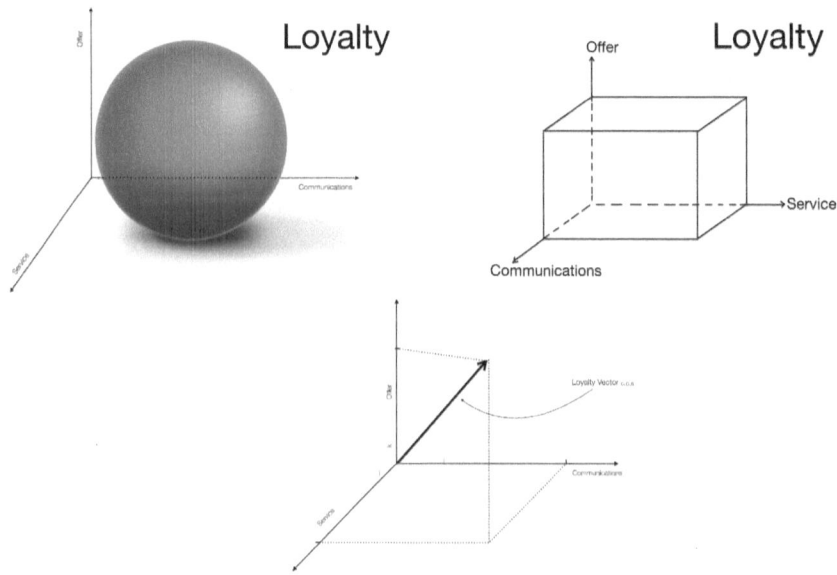

The journey from Loyalty Sphere to Loyalty Prism to Loyalty Vector.

No, nothing seemed to work. Even when the models were interesting, they lacked the capacity to communicate the final concept to a regular person. The idea of a model is to be clear, and my proposals didn't pass the test.

The sphere was appealing, yet it didn't convey the concept of independence between variables; a sphere grows on three dimensions, and it is not possible to express the effect of one dimension growing. If it happened, it would stop being a sphere, and loyalty had nothing to do with volume. Even being a nice idea, it didn't work, so it was

Bloop! Discarded.

The rectangular prism was a good solution for geometry lovers; loyalty was represented as the size of a box, which showed the effect of a single variable on the total size of it. Simple, yet complicated. Was loyalty a volume? What if the brand worked on just one or two variables? Rather than being a box, it would much better be a line or a square. It needed a lot of explanation in order to say something like: if you only work on one dimension, you'll get the loyalty line; if you work on two, you'll get the loyalty square; if you work on them three, you'll get the box, the parallelepiped! No, such a variable model would not sustain itself as an easy to remember tool, nor managers feel comfortable with it. So, it was:

Discarded, too.

The vector was an elegant approach to the model. It was proposed by one of my students, who was also an industrial engineer – like I am – and made it very easy to say something like: It doesn't matter how many variables you have; if one or more of them is different from zero, and has a size and direction, you'll have a resulting vector. It was a simple, elegant and easy to understand solution for graphing three variables, even if one or two of them were zero.

Accepted!

After several months of discussing it with my peers and colleagues, presenting it to different audiences, from business people to MBA students, I felt the model had some complications that made it difficult to explain, and took me lots of time to Wow! the audience. I didn't quite understand why, so I decided to keep the model like that, dealing with the audience the way every good communicator would do: Talking, drawing and giving examples until the audience got it. Exhausting, but it got the job done.

A brief detour to my personal life. I am a family guy who likes to get together with members of both my family and my wife's (who is, incidentally, also my partner on the marketing firm I founded back in 2001). My wife, Vini, has a very smart cousin, who is one of my most cherished in-laws, Akani. When we first met, Akani was a ten year old who fascinated me with his intelligence and eloquence, being able to hold a conversation about many interesting things way beyond his age.

Almost twenty years later, there was this family dinner where Akani was preparing his famous turkey; he and I started talking about things, and the COS Model came into the conversation. I started showing off, letting Akani know how smart my vector model was, how well it worked and represented reality, when Akani asked, knife-in-hand, the most important question I had from all the time reviewing the model:

So?

What do you mean by "so?", I asked. He smiled and said: What are you doing to make life easier for managers? How will this vector model be assimilated if it so hard to understand it for regular Joe? How will they measure the inputs? What is its relevance? What are the expected results?

Ditched! Boo!

Akani was right. The vector model was a nice, elegant model… if you were familiar with vectors and vector algebra. It used the i, j & k unitary vectors, and required the user to understand concepts such as magnitude, direction and angle; to make things worse, it needed all unitary vectors to be equal or greater than zero –the loyalty vector was not conceived to describe disloyalty, nor any other negative version of loyalty.

Zip. The vector model had to be discarded, and no other type of model was on sight to substitute it. What to do? Where to look for another representation of the model?

I tried, oh yes, I tried. I held conversations with graphical designers, with consultants, with managers, and the model got more and more complicated after each conversation. It was a vicious circle, where the need to understand vectors model made it hard to understand the model, so finding a clearer replacement was quite a task.

Until...

I was adding a new specialty to my career: Because of my work as a postgraduate teacher, I was selected to become a mentor on innovation and entrepreneurship. The national council for science and technology was launching these Innovation Nodes, where scientists and researchers were invited to help them find commercial applications for their inventions and findings. To be up to the task, I had to become proficient on methodologies such as Business Model Canvas, Lean Startup, Design Thinking, and the works of Steve Blank, the author of *The Four Steps to Epiphany*.

As an industrial engineer, back in college I learned soft systems methodologies, followed by others such as Blue Ocean Strategy –or the three generic strategies Michael Porter proposed on his classical book, *Competitive Strategy*: Cost leadership, differentiation and focus.

The mix of what I had to learn with what I knew, and putting it into practice with people from disciplines so different from mine, led me to a realization: The COS Model had to be drawn in a conceptual way –maybe not as accurate as a three dimensional vector– in such manner that a simple look at it might show the observer what is the brand doing to achieve customer loyalty. So, the COS Model Canvas was born, as a simple and effective tool to show the path to follow in the road to customer loyalty.

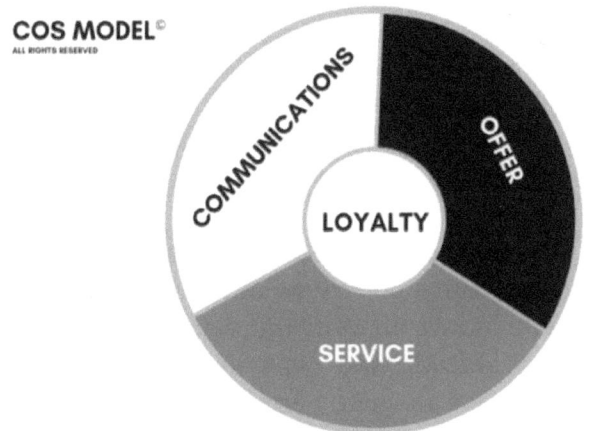

■ OKR, tactical plan, budget, key metrics.

☐ Communication plan, message, media plan, OKR, budget, key metrics.

■ OKR, tactical plan, budget, key metrics.

A good model represents reality as clear as possible, trying to include relevant elements and minimize noise; it is not a photograph; it is a depiction so clear the person reading it gets the idea in the simplest manner. The COS Model Canvas is designed to do it, relating loyalty with its quantitative and strategic elements –to manage something, you have to be able to measure it, remember?– using OKRs for each strategy –objectives and key expected results–, together with tactical plans, budgets and key metrics[1].

For example, let's start with a definition of what Loyalty may mean for a given company:

We define Loyalty as "to retain customers for at least five years, purchasing five times a year or more, with a Net Promoter Score of 56 or higher, and an average ticket per customer of $250 dollars or higher".

Yes, this definition is intended to cover what OKR states: set clear, quantitative objectives, and define what the key results will be– so we quantify our definition of Loyalty. It also includes attitude and behavior, as Dick and Basu recommend, so we are good here.

Now, let's think how the three strategies in the COS Model would look:

> Offer: We will guarantee a high, consistent service level, to ensure our customers always get what they buy from us.
>
> Communications: We will use bidirectional channels to keep a conversation open with our customers.
>
> Service: We will treat our customers as guests, to make them feel at home.

---

[1] To learn more about OKR's and how they are used at Google, go to my youtube channel, section Alive & Well, and watch *"Startup Lab workshop: How Google sets goals: OKRs"*

As you may see, these strategies are focused on achieving our objectives. We want frequent purchases, high satisfaction and repeated business. Be critical: Do you think customers who feel like guests, with an open conversation channel, and an impeccable offer, will remain loyal? I do. My experience says so. Try them. You have nothing to lose, and a lot to win.

If you are familiar with strategic thinking, you know how objectives are followed by strategies, then tactics and activities, supported with a budget and key metrics. Well, COS Model Canvas follows the same rule. From the objective, which is always Customer Loyalty –yes, always, this is what it was designed for– and three strategies to go for it, which are executed in the long term –it is common to implement the model for life– adjusting and updating them year after year until you reach and surpass the loyalty key results defined at the beginning, all of it supported with a budget fat enough to implement all the activities stated on the yearly plan, and the metrics to measure, manage and control your day to day operations.

The COS Model would operate in the same way: Companies implementing it would follow go down from objectives to multiyear strategies, to tactics, budgets and key metrics, to achieve their goal. Traditional strategic management put to work for a 21st century management tool.

TAKE AWAYS

Customer Loyalty is dependent on three variables: Offer, Communications and Customer Orientation. Your job is to choose which of them to use... or all three.

Good ideas from a team are not always the path to success. Strategic thinking and execution come in handy.

Whenever you think your ideas are the best, look for an Akani to ask you: So?

To implement the COS Model, be strategic: Think why, then what, then how will you do it.

Then, do it.

Trouble starts where and when you least expect it.

When at the top, the most probable way is downwards... be careful.

Have I told you about my friend Graham? He was a successful CEO who once got the prize for leading the best subsidiary on earth, got promoted and, ten years later, was asked to come back and deal with decreasing revenues, lost contracts and defecting customers.

This is his story.

Year 2000, Graham was the happiest CEO on earth. As general manager and president of the Mexican subsidiary, he received the Hubert trophy for being the most successful subsidiary worldwide of Hubert, a Fortune Global 1000 company he had worked for 20 years now. Together with the trophy came a promotion as VP, Latin America, which he happily accepted. His career was just like he had dreamt it.

He left his office in the hands of Larry, whose reputation as good country manager preceded him, since he had been in charge of a couple South American subsidiaries whose profits had been quite good during the past few years.

In the eyes of the corporation, Larry was successful at managing operations and keeping costs under control for many years. His profile seemed just right to continue the successful path Graham had opened for the company during his seven years as CEO.

But… life always seems to love putting a *but* in the way of successful organizations.

Yes, life sucks and *but* is never good news; good ol' Larry had this idea of solving everything cutting costs. From lowering the cost of hardware and equipment, to limiting how long and how frequent would the service calls to customers be, to limiting the length of customer contacts, all for the sake of saving money. In no time Larry decided to cut on service quality, no matter the impact on customer loyalty; for him, everything was about getting a healthy profit and loss statement for the short term, regardless of the long term-impact.

Larry's career as a CEO was not long, yet he was able to give the company the first punch on customers' satisfaction and loyalty. In a couple of years, he left, and left the company slightly wounded; those wounds were not fatal, yet Hubert was bleeding and beginning to lose customers. Jean Louis, his COO, who had been in charge since Graham times, was the most suitable candidate to succeed Larry.

Jean Louis. A guy with the nicest smile and the worst CEO style. After Larry, Jean Louis became the new CEO and did everything in his power to outdo Larry. Had Larry cut expenses? Jean Louis would do it better. Had Larry set limits on customer relations? Jean Louis would cut them to the ground.

Jean Louis did things as if his goal was to kill the company, which was now bleeding customers. In a short period, two to three years, customers contracts were down by 33%, and Net Promoter Score was 27 points down. The main reasons: loss of quality, price, and poor communication & service.

Everything Graham had built with his team to become the best subsidiary, had fallen under Larry and Jean Louis.
Satisfied customers fell from over 40% in 2000, to almost 25% on 2012, while unsatisfied customers five-folded from 2% on 2000, to almost 10% on 2012. A real crisis, fired up by Larry's and Jean Louis' management styles.

What to do? In the eyes of the corporation, the answer was quite clear: Bring back Graham to take the reins and get everything back in order. So they did, taking him back from his regional vice-presidency to assume, again, the country manager position.

Being a good soldier, Graham accepted the assignment without any complaints, and took matters into his hands.

Would he make it? Could he turn time back, to recover the company he left Larry a few years ago, and regain the conditions to be considered the number one subsidiary on earth? As they say...

It all starts with vision.

Graham had two great gifts: vision and management skills. He had the capacity to foresee trouble and opportunities, and the skills to turn them into advantages and strengths. Once back on charge, he started a thorough analysis and found things to fix, some urgent, some not, in order to reach again what he accomplished back in 2000.

First of all, he set a vision and published it: We will be market leaders in 2015, based on service excellence.

To be leaders, again. By 2015. Based on service excellence. Quite a goal, indeed.

He phrased it "Leadership through service by year 2015". Simple, clear, easy to understand, time bound. He published it and let everybody know what his vision was for year 2015.

Here's where Graham's life and mine got a common goal. As in any good story, there's always a moment when the guy in trouble finds the guy who has the means to turn that trouble into happily-ever-after endings... and these two guys were Graham and me.

Graham had a huge problem; I had a loyalty model. Like when the kingdom is in trouble and the peasant boy has a bag with just a slingshot and a few pebbles... Graham had a problem which my pebbles could solve, and I knew how to use his slingshot and pebbles to solve Graham's problem.

(This is the moment when I, as the narrator, take a step back and look at the complexity of the situation, asking myself: Am I being clear enough to let the reader understand how deep in trouble Graham is, and how timely my arrival is? "I think I

am, I tell myself" so I go back to telling the story, without any further doubts).

Graham and I meet for breakfast, together with Rupert, the chief commercial officer whose successful career at Hubert began just a couple of weeks before Graham's, so they had always seen themselves as a team. Rupert is the one who breaks the news to me. I listened carefully. Rupert's report on how things were at Hubert left me speechless, since they were way worse than I imagined. Then he asked me what they had to do to solve the problem. I told them about the COS Model, and they both went silent for a few moments.

After that silence, it was Graham who calmly said: We need your help. We need your model. We want to take Hubert back to be the best subsidiary, and it's a long shot. We need you to team up with us to take Hubert again to the summit.

I was overwhelmed. I knew what my answer had to be, and decided to breach protocol. Without consulting my partners, I said "Yes, we'll help Hubert get back to the top".

Just when trouble was at its peak at Hubert, the alliances to solve it were being signed at that moment, at a breakfast meeting somewhere close to headquarters, by three guys whose common goal was to turn things around.

They say heroes are not those who are fearless, but those who, in the face of danger, decide to take action overcoming their fears with the dream of victory. If this was the case, Rupert, Graham and I were heroes. We didn't know how difficult, how intense the fight in front of us was. We only knew we wanted to take Hubert back to the summit. Maybe that's what heroism is made of; vision and controlled fear.

· · · · ·

TAKE AWAYS

Heroism is made of vision and controlled fear.

Heroes are those who decide to take action in the face of danger.

If you are at the top, going down is quite easy. Your job is to not let it happen.

In the face of trouble, be calm and look for those who can help. Forget those who won't.

The story of three dreamers who wanted glory back.

> – Glory? No, I just want to be back at the top.
> – That's glory, sir.

Enterprise diagnostics, when done properly, are a great tool. They let you know what and who's wrong, and what's OK –for some strange reason, most analyses come up with lots of wrong things, and just a handful of things well done. Hubert's analysis was not the exception.

From a COO who loved to take every little decision in his hands, while leaving the important, big decisions to god-knows-who, to a number of customers complaining about unfulfilled promises, from deadlines to lack of communication, from bad service to bad spare parts planning, and nobody doing a thing to solve them, me and my team proposed Graham to take a simple path, which instead of cutting heads and punishing people, would take Hubert to recover customer trust and, therefore, their satisfaction and ultimately, loyalty.

Graham's vision of "Leadership through service by 2015" was published and became the foundation for defining three strategies based on the COS Model. The three heroes didn't know it then; teaming up had been a great decision.

Regarding offer, the strategy became "Impeccable offer", which meant customers were to get what they asked for, and the company would do everything to fulfill its promises on time. This strategy meant the company would have to improve on three dimensions: people, processes and technology. Simple, right?

People, as the main ingredient to deliver a service, are at the core of service, providing the human touch to the relationship between Hubert and its customers. It made sense to train people into soft skills such as customer oriented behavior, customer first, and assertive behavior – on a company with over 500 employees, nationwide.

People working on customer oriented behavior, customer first, and assertive behavior. Their enthusiasm was evident.

From communications came "Integrated Communications", meaning that Hubert would open the communications channels needed to have two way conversations with its customers, as the basic theory of communications says: Two parties sending and receiving messages, through a channel, in a common language, avoiding noise, sending feedback to let the other party know the message arrived in a clear manner.

The strategy had to focus on avoiding the typical "communication errors" that so often hurt relationships.

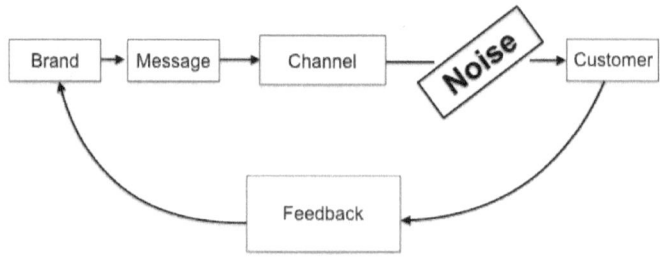

Communication cycle, as simple as it can be.

Last but not least –pardon the cliché– was the service strategy, or "Customer Orientation". It meant the whole company had to be oriented towards the customer, since everything would come as a consequence. Yes, Richard Branson says you have to first worry about your people, and they will take care of customers. For what me and my team found at Hubert, it is not always true. You may over-attend your people's needs and satisfaction, creating a comfort zone where your employees don't care anymore about the customers' wellbeing, since any changes would jeopardize their current status. Yes, Mr. Branson's concept was wrong in this particular case, and the team decided to do something: train the whole organization on how to be customer oriented, and create elements to help customers be at the very center of the operations, such as a customer service center with enough authority as to stop everything to help a troubled customer.

The Customer Orientation strategy might seem counterintuitive, yet it showed its great importance once the big 15 were identified and the organization needed to be up to their requirements –that's something we will address ahead in this story.

It was the beginning of a long, winding road, which will force much of the organization to change attitude, perspectives, ways of working and interacting with customers, while delivering the value they asked for. The trio didn't know it; it would take almost four years of hard, organized work to achieve the goal.

Some things are elementary.

The first thing to do after publishing the strategies was to plan the tactics and budget for year one. As they say, vision without implementation is hallucination – and one thing none of us had was lack of operational drive.

As executives, the three of us had careers where the right implementation was an important part of our success. From holding positions as financial, operations, commercial, marketing and chief executive officers, we had the collective experience to make it happen; and the first step to do so was to plan the yearly activities, establish a budget to accomplish them, and put together a good team.

For me it was an easy choice. My partner, Vini, is a smart, hands-on professional, with one outstanding skill: She makes things happen. Vini earned a bachelor's degree on psychology, and somehow it gave her the tools to motivate people and lead them towards the final goal, delivering results on time, within budget, and at the promised quality.

For Graham and Rupert, it was a little more complicated. Since they retook control, they had assigned their team members with extra responsibilities, which made availability a complicated issue. Nonetheless, they managed and assigned a team of three people – Pamela, Graham's former assistant, who knew customers very well; Jonah, the new marketing manager; and Andy, a human resources manager who had the most positive of attitudes. At the end, after going through all the challenges to implement the strategies, the choice proved to be the right one.

There was a lesson here: To make things happen, it is much better to assign regular, enthusiastic people with the right tools and authority, rather than optimal people with no resources. It happens to be elementary management, my dear Watson.

The leading team had a simple organization, too. I was in charge, reporting to Graham on a regular basis. Rupert stepped aside, turning back to his commercial duties, he was updated on the milestones and results in a less frequent manner.

It also proved to be a great decision. Instead of a committee, with lots of voices and opinions, a two-person managing team – three, since Vini was always there to provide support with facts, data and direct knowledge on the development of things– was the best way to reach the goals and remove obstacles from the way to results.

What happened? How did things go? What where the right decisions and the mistakes? How the team understood the way things were, before embarking on changing for the better?

Keep reading. Next chapter will take you through the implementation job; three years in a nutshell.

TAKE AWAYS

Get a Vision. Be enthusiastic at it.

To reach that Vision, set objectives, define your strategy, and the tactics to make it happen.

It is much better to have regular, enthusiastic people with tools, rather than the optimal ones with no resources.

A small leading team is much better than a committee.

Think and do ain't the same thing.

*Anybody can imagine great things;
only a few can make them happen.*

Day one arrived, and the team was excited. There were people to interview, customers to talk to, numbers to review, surveys to understand... the final objective was clear and challenging: To win back lost glory, growing customer loyalty, returning to the path of growth, and being again subsidiary number one. Simple.

Graham and Rupert gave Vini and me the names of all the members of Hubert's executive suite, and scheduled meetings with each one of them during the next couple of weeks. It was Christmas time, so we had to be swift; people would be gone for the holidays and we didn't have much time to waste before having all interviews.

First goal on each interview was to let the interviewee know what our team's objective was, to have them engage into a conversation where we could discuss three things: What had to be kept in order to make customers happy with Hubert's service; what had to be changed, and what had to be eliminated. No Hubert employees were in the interviewing team, to avoid political issues getting in the way of finding the truth.

It worked. Interviewees were open, and gave candid, professional opinions on how Hubert was doing about its customers.

Next step was to present findings and make decisions about where to start. The human resources manager, Andy –who was far from the stereotype about HR people not being strategic thinkers– proved to be a valuable ally... and an unexpected one, by the way. We'll talk about it later.

An action plan was drafted based on three things. Graham published his 2015 vision a couple of months before, and nobody seemed to be aware of it yet: The need to rectify things about customer satisfaction, and the need to turn numbers around, in two main indicators, Net Promoter Score and number of customers with one or more service contracts.

From the interviews and analysis, three things were identified as the root problems:

"Our customers don't get what they pay for".

"Customers don't know anything about us, nor we hear them".

"Service, and personal attention, are so poor, customers rather call the CEO to get their problems solved".

Wow! The three objectives and the three strategies fitted so well as if they were custom made for each other. Impeccable Offer; Integrated Communications; and Customer Focus were the way to go to accomplish the task.

After agreeing on the indicators to measure – NPS, customer retention index, and defection index – the operative plan and budget were prepared, all in record time. Clarity and urgency made a combination where going down from objectives to activities to budget took less time than expected, while getting rid of the back-and-forth reviews which come with this process. Looking back at it, maybe it was the reason for its success; a no-nonsense approach, where the goal was to have it up and running, paved the road to a results oriented budget, flexible and ready to work through the first year.

It was almost March, year one. The first quarter was already gone, and my team had a full year's objectives to accomplish. They had to do the steamroller approach: "When faced with bureaucracy, act as a steamroller, and go over obstacles. To get results, it is better to say sorry than ask for permission".

It worked.

The first thing was to train Hubert more than 600 employees on customer oriented behavior, nationwide. It had to be done in less than a month, and must deliver the corporation vision on how to treat the customer as king.

Let's pretend this is a commercial break, where the narrator says:

Hubert is an international corporation with a quality policy which says "do things right, from the first time, always". From its headquarters in ancient Europe, the corporation is proud to provide the highest quality from the very beginning, time after time.

[End of commercial break.]

No, Hubert's employees in the country were not aware neither about the policy nor the initiatives the corporation had put in place to accomplish it. It was on a sign everybody passed by when going in and out of the offices, without a second thought –much less deep thought.

What to do? The team's approach was simple. We would put together teams of up to 40 employees, for one day sessions, where we would deliver both theoretical and practical knowledge about customers, their needs, and how to serve them. It worked.

During those sessions, participants worked on three things: Learning about the corporation approach on customers and quality; discussing the quality policy; and proposing solutions to a case related to the situation at hand.

Ah, and a new answer was proposed as a tool to get out of complicated customer situations and requests in an elegant fashion:

"Yes, and…".

Yes, and… it turned to be the best concept to help employees, from service technicians to sales people, deal with customers' requests, because of the elegance it conveyed. "Yes", was what the customer heard so there was no way to feel mistreated or ignored; "…and" opened a door for finding next steps without compromising the relationship. It gave everybody the opportunity to look for help, to go to their bosses, to consult policies and procedures before going back with an answer which would go like: *Remember what you asked me? Well, this is what we can do to help.*

To help. The main purpose of having that training was to let the organization know they could help their customers solve their problems, satisfying their needs without getting into trouble with their bosses. It was an interesting change of approach which opened the road to what was to come next: Treat customers according to their value and needs.

We delivered 12 workshops in eight different cities throughout the country. It took lots of traveling for many people, complicated logistics to get people from either branches or field offices to the sessions on time, all with a tight budget and a strict schedule. It was worth the effort, and worked better than expected. More than 600 people from all over the country participated in this initiative, in record time. Andy's team was in total control of it, and when he made the post-seminar evaluations, he found that there was some valuable learning… it had to be put into practice soon, or it would be evaporated. So Andy called me and gave me a challenge: how to make all 600 put into practice what they just learned, without making it appear as an executive order?

The Three Friends.

My team had a characteristic. They were a marketing engineering team. They would innovate to solve marketing trouble, taking ideas from other areas of expertise, industries and previous experiences, in order to bring new solutions to the table.

In this case, the solution was a comic strip where three archetypical characters would tell stories about how to face troubled customers and complicated situations, all with a sassy spirit… we called them the Three Friends.

They were caricatures of three Hubert technicians, with clear personality traits. The business guy, pragmatic, results oriented, who wanted to put the company and interest before anything else.

The customer guy, optimistic, good natured, whose primary impulse would always be to put customers first, even at a cost to the company.

To tie them together, there was the control freak. The guy who always wanted to have everything under control, not letting a thing escape, and having an urge to tell everybody what to do, all the time. His interest was not with the business nor the customer; it was with the way things had to be done, to keep a tight ship.

Andy was an artistic guy, so he designed the original characters for The Three Friends. They were funny, inspired on true Hubert characters, and named with innocent, senseless names. *Friend, Compadre* and *Mate*, they were in charge of starring new adventures every week, to let Hubert's employees know how things go well when you put process, business and customers on the same level, without sacrificing any of them.

Once the message was delivered and reinforced, the organization was ready for the next step.

When he took office, Graham found he had a COO who was decision-averse. He'd rather let things pass until time solved them than making a decision; and the customers had realized it. He had a way to seem busy in front of people, just to avoid the real "busyness"; he could spend an hour with a minor customer, solving a much minor issue, instead of giving instructions to his team and focusing on the strategic and operational aspects of his duty.

This guy had been a branch manager during Graham's first "term", and a good one. A great example of Peter's Principle, his promotion was good for no one, and the customers paid the broken china, with a decline on service and quality which they were not liking. Customer defeat accumulated to over 25% during his tenure as COO.

Graham was a good man, nonetheless, and he decided to give his COO a second chance, so he gave him a choice He could either leave, or go back to that branch where he had been so successful. He chose the demotion (even when he got no deduction on salary; labor laws were strict on that and he was kind of safe) and moved back to where he was once successful; it was like moving from Mount Olympus to become a lesser god. Time would prove this was the wrong decision.

So, next question was where to bring a new COO from? There was nobody in the subsidiary who had either the credentials or the expertise to take care of the job, so

Graham decided to import talent. He got Flavio, who had been COO in the region's second most important subsidiary, with very good results on quality and customer satisfaction, to take care of the job.

In the meantime, Andy left the company. It was a major loss for the team, since he had been eager to help with things as the Three Friends, or writing motivational pieces for the company magazine, while being a great negotiator with the union, which was core to achieving success with the "Yes, and…" initiative. Finding a replacement for Andy became a long, tedious task, which made the team steer in a new direction to achieve results.

The solution was in the team. Pamela had been Graham's personal assistant for many years, and that gave her a deep understanding of who each customer was –even more when it came to valuable customers– and had a second attribute which made her quite the weapon the team needed: She had informal authority throughout the company, she was respected, her voice was listened, and her instructions were followed whenever she issued instructions about Customer requirements.

Now, the team was ready to implement tougher things. Jonah, the marketing manager, was an easygoing guy. He had a nice spirit and his ever-present smile made him an easy guy to deal with.

Jonah, Pamela, Vini and I were on the road to make major changes, while at the same time hitting major obstacles – like underestimating the power of corporate politics even when you are supported by the CEO, or trying to deal with an organization unwilling to move as fast as the situation called for. We managed to go around those and get the results we were after.

Results started to show.

"Vini, dear" said Pamela one morning, with that familiar tone she loved to use, "Graham wants to hear our proposal for the new Customer Service Center".

For a couple of months, Vini and Pamela had worked on creating a Customer Service Center where the most important customers would get an answer to their needs, regardless of the kind of need. Whether it was a problem, a request, or a simple question, the Center should be there to provide the necessary help. And so it was designed to do just that.

Staff, technology and processes to ensure 24 hours a day response, Monday thru Sunday, with no ifs nor buts. The Center would solve High Value Customers's requests in no more than 48 hours, regardless of the day they were reported... if Customers' operations never stopped, why would the Center do it?

Graham listened, asked, reviewed, and approved the proposal. The Center would have a staff of experienced people who were able to solve problems, not just report them, even going over other lesser value customers who were first in line. The Center would be equipped with communications technology to be sure no customer contact would go unnoticed. At the same time, the Center would have a very simple process, which began with a customer contact, and finished with its solution in less than 48 hours.

The Center had to be operational in less than a month following approval. It meant Vini and Pamela had to pull, push and force lots of things to be ready on time. The IT guys, the phone services company, the Human Resources department… everybody responded to the beat of the drums, and delivered on time. "Yes, and…" proved again to be the best answer. It led to solutions instead of reasons why not.

In the meantime, Graham and I were making a thorough analysis of customers' revenue and earnings during recent times, to define an 80-20 Paretto distribution, looking for the very best customers… and a surprise was awaiting.

Hubert had about 3,700 individual customers, which amounted to approximately 11,000 contracts. Graham and I were expecting that some 750 customers would be generating 80% of the profits, and we had no idea how wrong we were.

Paretto's principle states that 80% of results come from roughly 20% of causes. In this case, both Graham and I were betting that it was the case that most profit or revenue would come from a fraction of customers… boy, we were as wrong as you can be in all good stories, and it played well on our favor.

Fourteen customers generated almost 30% of Hubert's profits. 15 customers. It didn't matter Paretto was useless to even make an educated guess about it; the number happened to be a blessing.

A blessing? How come?

Vini was in charge of the creative team. She had been working with some of her team members to develop a proposal to send a direct message from Graham to high value customers, in order to communicate the new Customer Care Center. And they came up with a symbolic, simple proposal: The Red Phone.

A red phone is a strong symbol. Batman has a direct line with Commissioner Gordon; The White House and The Kremlin were linked by a Red Phone; even the Power Puff Girls had a red phone with the mayor. People understand the meaning and importance of such a device, and it was proposed as a communications piece to be sent to high value customers to let them know about their importance to Hubert and its Customer Care Center – created with an exclusive telephone number, a dedicated crew, and the authority to solve problems, needs and requests way better than the normal channels– using a memorable piece, at the same time practical and good looking, so customers would feel nice when getting it.

Vini and her creative team devised a Red Phone to deliver the message to Hubert's customers.

They designed the Red Phone as a flash memory, so it would be a useful tool for customers, to tell them about the immediate communication capabilities. It was loaded with a video from Graham where he announced the creation of the Customer Care Center, dedicated to "you, our most valuable customers", making the formal naming of Pamela as the Customer Care Manager, and sharing the center's direct telephone numbers in a confidential-like manner.

The Red Phone was a success. Some customers even applauded when they got it. It looked and felt like a high-quality item – designed in Mexico, and manufactured in China. The result was spectacular, beautiful and simple.

When recipients plugged the flash memory into their computers, there came Graham on a video where he, looking straight into the camera, would say: "Our purpose at Hubert is to deliver quality, from the first time, always, and so we have created the Customer Care Center, under Pamela Mattison's command, whose job is to satisfy your requests, either they be for service, help or a simple request, in 48 hours or less", with a superimposed text with the legend "Pamela Mattison, 555·555·1234".

To give a fun touch, after a short pause, Graham's lines finished by saying "this is not an impossible mission; this message will not self-destroy, so you can access it whenever you need to", with a Mission Impossible-like song in the back ground.

Red Phones were delivered to every decision maker on the top 15 customers, now known as "Red Phone Customers". The organization started using that name when referring to an important customer, without using acronyms nor contractions. The full name stuck, because using it conveyed the power of a customer whose weight was big enough to drive strategic decisions.

It was looking great, and the toughest part was yet to come. As any good business story, this one is full of jealousy, treachery and unexpected enemies, and I'll tell you later about them.

. . . . .

TAKE AWAYS

Thinking is the first step. Execution has to come right after.

Don't bet on Paretto's 80-20.

When creating your top customer service team, look for experienced, customer oriented people.

Get rid of decision averse people. They are harmful.

Things you'll see, dear Sancho.

> *'Welcome to my world; it is full of beautiful, deceptive things', said the Frog.*
> *And it was.*

Two new arrivals complicated things for the team. Stewart, the new human resources manager arrived, and he was eager to show how he knew the right way to do things. Graham had met him in his previous job at an engineering company, when he managed to convince him about how good he was... yet time would show how misled we were.

Since his arrival, he tried to demonstrate how everybody else was to blame for things. He loved meetings and writing minutes where everybody else had something to do, just to obstruct the team's efforts and make things fail so he had someone to blame.

So Vini and I had to set a new action plan, a much-needed plan B, which meant I would be the one dealing with Stewart, attending his meetings, helping him edit and write his in-company magazine... while Vini was in charge of doing whatever was in the original plan to finish that first year as scheduled.

Stewart proved to be a menace for the project and jeopardized it several times; from trying to take ownership of the Three Friends, to launch his own First Class Program, an initiative based on a great idea... and the poorest execution possible: It was meant to heighten the spirits of installation and maintenance teams throughout the country... it ended up being a prize for those who were nice to Stewart, without any relation to their performance or results.

The team went on stealth mode. Since HR had nothing to do with customers, the decision we made was not to do any training nor internal communications beyond Customer Oriented Behavior training, and "Yes, and... " attitude. Political war is not something you want when trying to get something done under a tight schedule.

After some weeks, I brought the issue up in a conversation with Graham. "Stewart's doing everything he can to undermine our job, Graham", I told him.

Graham stood silent for a while, looking out the window. Vini held her breath and I doodled on my notebook.

After an eternity –remember time relativity?– Graham turned around and said "You know? His honeymoon is almost over, and he has to show results soon. Be patient."

The team had been patient, indeed, and he was asking us to do so for more time. "OK, we will, and we will need your help soon", Vini said on that calm, firm voice she used when things got serious.

It proved to be a complicated task. Stewart managed to delay small things in such manner that my team would be perceived as lazy, unable to deliver. I was assigned to take charge of the relationship, knowing it was a situation where I needed emotional intelligence as a critical weapon... as it happened to be.

Every single piece, every detail, every idea was challenged. If I proposed an article for the company blog, everything in it was criticized, and sent back for "review, again". If it was a photo, the angle, light, composition, framing, people on it were points of discussion.

The team learned to work under those conditions and things got much better. Keeping an eye on the ball, in this case supporting the Impeccable Offering strategy, we devised ways to create options so one could be sent as a decoy, just to send the right one after the expected refusal came. It was a great decision, since adapting one's way of working to the customers' style is one of the most challenging situations when providing professional services.

Training slowed down to almost zero activity, so our team focused on the other two strategies, mainly the Integrated Communications one, and kept the hard work. Since the Red Telephone had been such a success, the next step started to be planned: Delivering value to the customers in the form of things which might be useful for their day-to-day activities, such as training, information, or other tools to support their results as executives and decision makers.

There's this Mexican saying *"Man proposes, God disposes, the Devil comes and everything decomposes"*. Customer loss was lowering and pointed towards reversion, when someone in the Corporate headquarters decided it was time for a "Portfolio protection" campaign. The idea was to develop a roadshow to explain what the portfolio was, the impact of losing such portfolio, and how to avoid it.

Even when it was supposed to be handled by Human Resources, the Quality Manager made a swift movement and convinced Graham to let him be in charge, a guy who was known by his focus on getting things done right, even if it meant to run over one of his peers. He came from the auto industry, and had a strong background on things regarding quality: Measuring it, discussing its implications, and educating about it.

Portfolio Protection turned out to be a nice challenge. It meant to hit the road again and talk with all of Hubert's employees, discussing what portfolio was, how much it meant on profit terms, and how to avoid customer loss – portfolio was the name for service contracts, so it was core to Hubert's business: more than 63% of its profit was generated by portfolio customers, so protecting them was a matter of financial health, if not life and death.

With a very simple cartoon, where a guy was trying to keep water into a barrel full of holes, the idea of how customers were lost was transmitted. It was a funny and clear message, and people understood it quite fast, getting ready to the real question: How to avoid the leakage?

Portfolio protection was a nice initiative, mostly informative. The idea was to communicate the impact on Hubert's numbers of losing customers, and its intention was not to get any other results. As many corporate initiatives, they are incomplete, and focus on small details, losing sight of the big picture, in this case the loss of customers Hubert Mexico had suffered for so many years was not in the programs cross hairs.

Graham had managed to deliver good numbers to the corporation; although results were not as good as back in 2000 when the Hubert Trophy was awarded to Mexico, he was a manager who knew how to turn things into profit even in the face of adversity, so he took corporate pressure away from the real challenge: His 2015 vision. Corporate offices had not yet sent any signal about customer loss, and Graham wanted to keep them as far from his back as possible, so he got to the point of micromanaging in such manner that he reported good numbers and his bosses were calmed.

Some things change overnight, and an unexpected call from Hubert's CEO came: Mr. Hubert had just got a phone call from a small customer back in central Mexico, who was complaining about a project gone wrong. He told Mr. Hubert that, if the company didn't deliver on a certain date just six weeks away, he'd go to the newspapers and social networks to let everybody know about Hubert's lack of commitment and failure to keep its word.

Crisis!

Graham summoned operations, marketing, installation services –my team was considered part of marketing, so we were called in too– and customer service. It was a harsh meeting, since Graham had just had a conversation with Mr. Hubert, who gave him just one, plain order: "Fix it. You have two months".

The installations manager, who was responsible for the problem –he had given the customer his word three times– showed no guilt. I, on the other hand, saw an opportunity to do something regarding both the Impeccable Offering and the Customer Orientation strategies, and spoke out my thoughts: What if we train all employees on what Red Telephone is, its implications and processes?

Jonah, the marketing guy, gave me a look of complicity, so I continued giving my reasons. "If we take this chance, we will use a crisis as an excuse for letting everybody know what a Red Telephone customer is, what are the business implications of this name, and how to act. It is THE opportunity to turn the Red Telephone into a core attitude, **a core value** for Hubert Mexico's employees" (yeah, I emphasized the words "a core value" when I said them).

Graham smiled. Jonah, who also had an acute sense of business, agreed. Pamela started giving too much importance to potential obstacles, and the installations manager babbled some words which no one cared about.

"You have six weeks. Can you do it?", Graham asked.

"Yes, sir, we can", I said, looking at Jonah, who smiled and said "Yes sir, we will do it, even with the tight schedule". Vini, who was in charge of operations, gave me a "you better be right" look and, true to her nature, started thinking how to get things done.

Graham left the room and the team stood still for a few seconds –the installations manager, who disappeared without a sound, soon to be forgotten by the others– just to start putting an action plan together…

...and boy, we did. The team managed to get a plan where in four weeks we would get all employees trained, after a two weeks preparation period, when we would get copies, materials, props, promotional articles, presentations, and logistics ready to deliver the message: *There's 15 Red Telephone customers, they are above everybody and everything else, and we will act accordingly.*

Red Telephone customers are above everybody and everything.

Three weeks after that meeting, the first group met at Hubert's training facilities. Me and my team –which included Bernie, Veronika, Annie and Steff– were ready to begin. We had created a Red Telephone logo which was imprinted in T-Shirts, wristwatches and posters that were to be delivered to each session's participants.

One particular message caused a deep impression on participants. We agreed Jonah would interrupt me just when I was to name the 15 Red Telephone customers – who accounted for almost 30% of profits– with a sad expression, saying: "No, Lalo, they are 13. We just lost La Fayette Group". It was true; La Fayette cancelled all of its contracts with Hubert a few days before the training began, and impact on profit was hard: Without this revenue, profit was expected to go down between two and three percent points by the end of the year.

I used this as an argument to stress how important Red Telephone customers were, and why the organization had to fight with teeth and claws to keep them, even against the organization's own policies. At the end of the session, all employees signed a poster where a big Red Telephone was imprinted, wearing their T-Shirts and wristwatches with the Red Telephone logo on them, as a sign of their commitment to keeping customers satisfied.

These sessions were delivered in record time; the team finished the assignment in five weeks total, together with the problem that originated this. The angry customer received his installation in fewer weeks than those offered by the CEO, and he withdrew his threat. Graham made sure everybody knew about this, as a final reward for being so fast on delivering and taking the Red Telephone sessions.

In the mean time, Flavio was doing a great job implementing the Impeccable Offer strategy. He named managers for all offices, made sure people were aware of and knew how to perform all the activities the customers expected according to their contracts, and made sure simple elements such as tools, software, and equipment were ready for each member of the operations area, in order to perform excellent, impeccable work. He had to be tough; the former COO who Graham had demoted to branch manager was replaced, and two new branches were opened, based on variables as committed response time and number of customers on the region.

Customers started noticing the difference. It was not enough yet; a few more things had to be done.

TAKE AWAYS

It is your job to bring HR on board.

Some customers are more valuable than others; find out who they are.

Treat customers according to their value and needs.

Identify your 80-20 customers; the list will surprise you.

Yes, and…

> *When you answer "Yes" in a negotiation, you disarm your opponent by not opposing what you've been asked. Following it with an "…and…", opens the door for new conditions, convenient for both sides.*

Customers were still not happy with Hubert's service, and employees were struggling to achieve the objective levels on customer satisfaction.

It was clear what to do. We needed the whole corporation to feel the joy of treating customers as the best thing ever, so Graham accepted to embark us in a challenging trip: to get the Customer Excellence Certification before Brazil. It was tough, seeing how bad some things were across the organization, and it was worth the try.

We had also to start a crusade to win back lost customers, and strengthen relationships with those still on board, so we devoted our efforts to a three-elements mission: Recover the lost sons; fix whatever customers thought was broken; and win the Customer Excellence Certification by year's end.

It was the best challenge possible. It was both tough and doable. Me and my team were assigned with the task of preparing the strategy for items two and three, and helping turn Lost Sons task force into an actionable campaign.

And it took us a full year to achieve the goals.

A full year.

Getting back those customers who left because of dissatisfaction, is a hard thing. There's broken promises, loss of trust, and many other feelings that spoiled the relationship, so restoring it is a hard thing to do.

We decided we would go after lost customers, and we would succeed doing it. So, let me start by explaining what the Lost Sons task force was and how it worked.

When customers leave because they don't get what they believe they deserve for the money they pay, there's a sense very similar to betrayal. People feel like they were cheated on, and it hurts, making it hard to convince them to come back. If you have ever known somebody whose sentimental partner cheated on, you know what the feelings are.

Now, imagine we decided to put on our best smile and go back to those customers, saying something like a "please forgive me, I will not do it again ever". We knew it had to be just a small part on a bigger, professional offer. And we did it. Together with Jerome –the contracts manager who had been with the company more than ten years– we got the agreement from both operations and CSC on how they would respond to customers who decided to come back. We put them down on writing and there we went, armed with three things: an apology, an offer on how day to day operations would flow –including service levels, response times and penalties if they were not met– and the process on how to get service like a Red Telephone customer, even if they were not (yes, maybe they were small, yet our decision was to bring back as many customers as possible, and Hubert was willing to give them these privileges).

A small task force was put together to work as a commando. As I said before, they were in a crusade, on a rescue mission, so they were set apart from the main sales force. Their goals, their measurement and compensation were different, since velocity was an important element; time was running and the Lost Sons task force needed to show it could be successful.

When it was the turn for strengthen relationships with customers, we took an example from Steve Blank, and went on a customer discovery trip.

Customer discovery is a simple and powerful way of setting the right value proposition: go to your customers segments and ask them about what their pains are regarding what you do for them; what the benefits they expect from what you deliver; and how their jobs are benefited or damaged by what you do and how you perform.

We went to talk with three top notch customers. I led the dialog, and we filmed it to later show it to employees. We didn't expect it; the insights we got from those interviews were very powerful.

An old saying goes "Don't tell me, show me". So we did. We didn't tell Hubert's employees how things were; we let them listen to customers and find out by themselves. They listened to the customers' unedited answers to questions about how satisfied they were about such things as service, invoicing, customer service, or people itself. People could listen to answers where customers said "I have not switched to your competition because one particular technician fixes our equipments, as he did for my father when he was in charge; except from him, nobody else in Hubert cares about satisfying our needs".

Showing this was a real bomb. We shook people's convictions and certitudes with their performance, letting them know by their customers own words how bad they were doing.

Yes, and…

…we announced the second part of this plan: We will get the Customer Excellence Certification by late October, way before Brazil could do it.

It was a challenge. It meant we would pass several tests on how processes were in place, and how people knew how to perform according to them, and pass an audit about it. It became a challenge that, at the end, costed Stewart his job. The poor guy's managerial skills were not up to the task.

Being headless on HR was a complication. Jonah had just earned his MBA from the top business school in Mexico, so he was fully prepared to take care of the job –even when he was *just* the marketing guy.

The strategy to win the Certification was quite simple. All of Hubert's employees would earn it. No single area would champion it, no individual would be in charge, but each and every employee of Hubert. It seemed like one of those enthusiastic, far fetched, useless things we see everyday, and it had a difference, a huge difference: Its execution was impeccable.

Remember Hubert's quality motto? Do things right, from the first time, always? Well, we applied it also to the certification, and things became easier.

We trained everybody on the company on the Customer Excellence ideals, processes and objectives. Jonah made sure everybody attended the videoconferences, and had the required take aways to be aligned with the certification.

On the other hand, our team worked together with Graham, creating the Customer Excellence Ambassador Corps, which was made out of people selected at random from different areas and levels, with the authority to lead and make decisions regarding customer excellence. Since ambassadors work under what's known as the Chancellory, Vini and I proposed to create a Customer Excellence Chancellor position, and gave this title to Graham, who accepted it with joy –yes, I know there was some business malice behind the proposal, and we needed someone with heavyweight to lead the effort, and no one better than the CEO.

Yes, my bad ;-)

The Customer Excellence Ambassadors, or Ambassadors, as they were known, made a great job as the proud guardians of Hubert's processes and attitudes towards customers, and it paid off very well.

We failed the initial audit and test. Flaws, faults and missing things gave us a low score. Yet, our spirits went way up. The Chancellor let everybody know where had we failed, reinforcing Jonah and the Ambassadors' position in regards of the Certification, so everybody went back to training, studying and doing their homework to achieve the certification. (By the way, Brazil made a terrible mistake. When they heard about Mexico failing the audit, they paced down, and time proved it to be the worst decision for them –and that's a different story).

Two months later, at the end of September, auditors came back, and the audit was flawless. Processes, tasks, people, everything was above the expected levels, and Hubert Mexico won the certification in record time.

People were ecstatic. When teams work hard to win, and do it, there's a sense of gratification which is hard to explain and great for business. It was the case, and things turned around right away.

A few months later, fiscal year closed and results were great. Not just good, great.

NPS had gone up from 28 to 53.

Customer retention had been successful and customer loss was below 10% again.

General revenue and profits were above plan.

Headquarters were happy. Not only regional, world headquarters too. It meant we had accomplished our mission, with a plus: Graham was re-appointed vice-president for the Latin American region at Hubert. The main reason? The corporation wanted him to lead other subsidiaries to achieve the same things he did in Mexico.

Was my team responsible for the success? Yes. As everybody else in Hubert, 'cause we just did the planning based on the COS Model, Graham's vision and Jonah's enthusiasm, working hard for months to get the job done.

It is a story like all stories had to be: A challenge, a group of people willing to face it with valor and hard work, and a happy ending.

. . . . .

TAKE AWAYS

Yes, and...

If you have a great challenge, team up with your people to face it.

Failing is not something to fear, but to build upon.

In business, winning is a team thing.

And they rode off into the sunset.

What happened, Daddy? Does the story have a happy ending?

Jonah's career took a fast pace after he got his MBA. Today, he is Mexico's CEO at a Forbes Global 500.

Graham retired and became an independent consultant. He helps companies from other industries which serve the same market. He's successful and happy.

Flavio moved back to Brazil to become CEO of the Brazilian subsidiary of Hubert. His successor deals with stories about him every day.

Rupert retired. He is the proud grandfather of three and spends most of his days enjoying his new role and plays golf with former customers. His successor asked him to be his coach. He refused.

Pamela is now Director of Customer relations at Hubert. Jerome reports to her.

Stewart switched careers. He is now a motivational speaker and writer, and he gets to enjoy his family a lot more… when he is not abroad.

The team moved to work at other projects, with the same joyful spirit.

I got my PhD.

PART TWO. The magician gives away his tricks.

If I tell you, it wouldn't be magic.

The kid thanked him and smiled.
Now he knew his magic would be alive for ever...

Let's play a strategy game. Imagine you have one problem, three goals to achieve, and three strategies to do it. How will you act?

The problem is we want our customers to keep purchasing from us for a long time, without having to worry about our competition's efforts to take them away. Your goals are clear and challenging. Minimize customer turnover; increase satisfaction; grow average revenue.

To tackle them, you and your team devised three strategies. Impeccable offer; integrated marketing communications; customer focus. They are not slogans; you chose them because you want to differentiate your company from your competition and make customers have a clear and sound reason to stay.

How to make those strategies work? As you are aware, strategy is a lot like a magician's tricks: We see what he is accomplishing, and we will never know how he did it.

Let me tell you about the magic and what to do to make it happen. I will begin by telling you this is a managerial book. It means it is intended to provide managers –no, I will not go into the manager-leader false dilemma– tools to make those objectives a reality, killing the "Loyalty is dead" myth in the way there, which is this book's final goal.

Customers give us their trust. They expect to receive something of value in exchange for their money, and when they do they feel satisfied. Satisfied customers are prone to two things: To keep buying, and to tell others about us. Both things are good for business, so our point of departure is a question, a design question: How do we ensure our customer satisfaction?

It is not a marketing question. It is is not a rhetorical question. It is an operational question, involving the whole organization, and whose answer resides at the very heart of our business model.

Let's imagine we are a bread company. What do our customers expect from us? Is it fresh bread, every day, so they can have dinner at night with warm croissants and crusty *bolillos*[2]?

It is when strategic thinking becomes operational, following a straightforward approach. Once you set your objectives and strategies, you have to define three things: Tactics, budget and control tools.

Let's begin with the tactical thinking. It all comes from one question, what do we have to do to give our customers what they expect from us? Let's call it the operational question.

---

[2] Bolillo is a Mexican piece of bread; it refers to approximately six inches of wheat bread, golden, crusty, and soft in the inside, great for stuffing, cutting, slicing or dicing; it's by far my favorite.

And this is an operations matter, which is answered by a triangular model. People, processes and technology.

The Impeccable Offer model.

People. Those who we call employees, associates, team, are the people in charge of making things happen. It doesn't matter if you are on the physical or the digital world, or both. People have to deliver your promises to your consumers, according to what the consumers want. People have to be ready to take over the task and make it a successful one, time after time after time...

Have you ever been to a McDonalds, a Starbucks or the Ziva Hotel in Puerto Vallarta? What did you see as the common denominator?

Let me tell you a story. Last spring I spent my wedding anniversary trip at Ziva, and service was great. Being as I am, I looked for the manager and complimented him on how good the hotel's staff service was, and asked what he did to achieve it. "Training, lots of training, and we still have at least another year to go to get to the level of our sister hotel in Cancun", he answered with a smile.

Wow!

He was not only humble, he had it quite clear. He knew people need training to acquire the needed skills, and the reinforcement to make them part of their daily behavior, as it takes years, not weeks –much less a "one day design thinking seminar"– to define the path and achieve the desired results.

Developing people's knowledge, attitude and skills is a long term effort, and you have to start somewhere. The first part is to let everybody know what their role is on answering the operational question.

Answering an operational question requires processes to be designed, mapped, established, or whatever is needed to be sure we know everything happening from beginning to end while giving our customers what they expect from us.

I've heard people say "I hate processes, they are bureaucratic". Good news: most of your customers will remain with you if you give them what they want, time after time. Bad news: the only way known to modern organizations to deliver in a standard manner is to design processes and stick to them. Sorry.

Back to business, a process is a recipe. A protocol. A how-to guide. We've done them for centuries, and somehow we dread them when it comes to implementing them on organizations. Let's answer our operational question with a recipe, a protocol, a how-to guide, and make sure we are able to provide our customers that fresh bread day after day so they may have dinner with a crusty *bolillo* and a steamy croissant.

What do we have to do to ensure this? It starts way before the bread gets to our customers' table. It begins with the planning process, with the preparation to have all the ingredients and inputs required to set up the oven, to prepare and cook the dough, to pack the bread and stock it, to deliver it to the stores and let it be on the shelves right on time for our customers to buy it and bring it home.

Is it challenging? You bet!

I am an industrial engineer by training; processes are at the core of my education; while I might be a little biased it doesn't matter, since processes are at the core of all businesses. Let me give you an example:

You are preparing your weekly production schedule, and you prepare to deliver 10,000 daily bolillos and croissants to your stores. What do you have to do?

Take your tablet and stylus – or paper and pencil if you wish– and let your imagination flow, dealing with all aspects of production , stocking and delivery that have to do with completing your task: 10,000 bolillos per day per store (by the way, you have to have a quantitative goal; otherwise, you'll be just wandering about, lost in the dark).

Go. Fetch your iPad, your dear Moleskin, your Excel spreadsheet, and start thinking hard about it; from what you need to get, to what you need to do, and whatever must happen in between.

I'll wait for you right here...

...ready?

What did you find? Which elements did you find as relevant for achieving your goal? Now, let's create an algorithm –remember, it's the 21st century and we just love the word.

Write a number one, a period and a dash. What's your first task?

Your second?

Third?

Are there any decisions you have to make based on current conditions, such as day of the week, or holidays, or a truckers' strike?

Go all the way down until the bread is delivered to the store on time and ready for your customer to arrive and purchase it. Think on how you will charge for your product, how you will promote it to generate demand and let your customers know about any new offers you may have...

It doesn't matter if your list was long or short. It doesn't matter how technical nor what you language was. It doesn't matter if you used an iPad or a yellow pad.

You know what's the only thing that matters? That the whole team in charge of preparing your bolillos and delivering them on time know it by heart and act according to it. Every single time. Period.

The rest is not important.

See my point now?

An algorithm is not just a piece of paper in a Trapper Keeper, nor a piece of software in Amazon's servers; it is a documented process where we define who does what and when in order to fulfill an operational question, which comes from a strategic question. Remember? First, we asked what the customer wanted, and then we asked what did we have to do in order to deliver it. The algorithm, the process is our most important tool, since it guarantees our service will be provided with equal quality every time. It states the answer to "who does what, when and where?": They do that, then and there.

Have you seen the movie "The Founder"? It is the story of Ray Kroc, who led McDonalds to become the company it is today. Well, there's this term, McDonaldization, and it comes from Kroc's obsession with processes and doing everything the same way, everywhere, all the time. It is not a coincidence they are known as a company with such standard products that even The Economist has an index to identify world currencies over or under valuation called the Big Mac Index: It estimates currencies value according to how much a sandwich is worth in local money on different countries... and it works because a Big Mac is always a Big Mac.

Do you get my point now? The trick for doing things right, the first time, always, is defining processes, letting everyone know them, and working in accordance. Please, keep it to yourself, since you don't want neither your competitors nor any entrepreneurs who think an app is a company to realize this: Processes are the secret for delivering standardized, good products and services time after time, and getting satisfied customers.

Now, the second trick.

Remember the operations question? As a second element of it, we have the communications question. It arises right from the Integrated Communications strategy: "how do we communicate with the customer?".

Yes, I know, this is the immediate communications era, and everybody is connected, having a voice, and listening to everybody else, using either digital, direct or mass media.

But (and, as my cousin Betty says, "a 'but' kills what came before"): If your customers are hyperconnected and hypercommunicated, it doesn't matter, because it is your obligation to make sure there is a communications cycle between you and them, and yes, it is your job to manage it.

It is your job to manage your communications cycle (am I crystal clear?).

Going back to basics, let's talk about the communications cycle. Let's go Communications 101, and revisit that good ol' concept of sending a message from a sender to a receiver, through a channel, using a code, overcoming noise to get a response back. Remember it?

Well, from now on, you are going to own it. Yes, I am well aware about what I'm telling you. Forget all the hype about digital age communications being on the side of the consumer, and brands just listening to try to make some sense.

As brits would say, it's bullocks.

Why?

Because you just can't afford to let communications between you and your customers be out of your control. If you are opening a channel between you and your customers, you are going to own it, to control it, to be responsible and accountable for whatever happens with it. If you are not willing to do so…

> *…do not open a communications channel.*
> *Period.*

Do you get my point? It's so simple it sometimes becomes hard to understand.

Let me go back one step and tell you about my reasons.

Adopting a strategy such as "Integrated Communications" means a huge commitment with your customers, since you will have to use different channels to deliver them a consistent message, taking care of making them not contradictory nor hard to understand, while at the same time differentiating the copy for each customer segment to get it.

For example. You may define you will use mass media, direct and digital. So you prepare an ad to publish it on a trade magazine your customers read. Then, you open a Twitter account, to tweet and open an interaction door with your market. Last, you launch an email newsletter, which will get to your customers every two weeks, and a call center, where they can reach you via phone, email and WhatsApp.

That's too many communication channels, you know? Will you risk not being able to react when some customer tweets a complaint, or sends an email back asking for help, or gets in touch with your contact center to look for a new product?

What if, on the other hand, you want to reach your customers with different messages, tailored according to their specific behavior or needs? Will you risk getting those messages mixed up, and having a low value customer calling to get the ultra prime offer you created for high profitability customers only?

You have to control what you tell, to whom, and when. You must control which channels are available to which customers. You have to control what are you going to answer, to whom, when and how. You can not lose control of your media and the way you use it to get in touch with your customers, either individual by individual, segment by segment, or massively.

Do you get my point? Forget those voices telling you 21st century made us lose control of your communications channels; be the owner of your messages and grasp them with a firm hand, so you can control them and your messages (remember the definition of control? It's goes like "... to keep things on a desired state, and if they get out of it, bring them back").

So, remember, you have to control your communications. And control is a part of a management process, where you plan, you execute and you control. So, the initial strategy for your plan is simple: use integrated communications. Then, define the tactics, budget and control variables to keep it running and...

...execute. Make it happen.

See? It is quite straightforward. Let me give you my advice on how to turn the Integrated Communications strategy into an actionable plan:

First, define a media plan, stating which media are you willing to use to reach each customer segment, and how often do you want to use them in order to get the holy grail of communications: reach and frequency.

Those media can be traditional as a magazine, newspaper or TV commercials. It doesn't matter, because you will define them according to your customers segments' profiles and preferences.

Second, make a budget. Get a committed amount from your finance area, your boss, your board of directors, saying how many dollars will you be able to spend during the fiscal year to keep contact with your customers. A rule of thumb is to spend around 1/50th and 1/30th of your target customers' yearly revenue on communications with them. No, it's not a random number; a $150,000 per year customer may get a $3,000 to $5,000 yearly budget for communications (including agency fees, the media budget, and any gifts you may give your customers), which is good enough to be in touch every year and have an active ear with it. Yes, you are a manager, so it is your duty to get those dollars to work; if you ask for more, you won't get it; if you ask for less, it will be useless.

So, don't be shy and go get the budget.

Third, once you have an authorized budget, revisit your media plan. You will have to make decisions on which media to keep, which media to let go, and it will be an executive task, simple and boring, core to your strategy. Yes, you have to have integrated communications and you only have so much money; be brave, manager up, and make the necessary decisions to make it happen.

Fourth –and as important as it can get– define your control process and key performance indicators.

A control process is core to achieving your results. Have you heard about how things "went out of control", whenever there's a messy situation?

No, the problem is not letting them out of control, the problem is not being able to get them back in order… and that's your job, as a manager. To keep things under control most of the time, so you can achieve your goals, sticking as much as possible to the plan.

See?

Now you are ready for the creative part, defining the communications, messages, slogans and specific pieces to send your customers, using the media your plan stated, with the frequency and reach you chose, in order to get four things:

The right message,

to the right customer,

at the right time,

thru the right channel.

Simple, yet quite complicated to execute, since managers rarely perceive communications as something they have to manage, and more like an advertising agency responsibility – by the way, if you want to use an agency, it is OK, just keep in mind always that you are the manager, you are responsible for keeping communications with your customers alive and well, and you are accountable for the communications results.

There's a third trick, remember?

I've already given you two tricks, one about delivering your customers what you offered, and the other about being in touch with them. The third one is the simplest, yet the most complicated to achieve.

Ready?

Treat them like royalty.

When I first talked in depth about loyalty with female customers, one recurrent expression was: "so they treat me as a queen". Going deeper into its meaning, it turned to be a very logical wish, where customers expressed their vision on what they deserved for their money.

Money is hard to make. Once a person decides to let it go in exchange for something, the typical expectation is high quality or, at least, being treated as someone special. No, it has nothing to do with the product or service itself; it has to do with our nature. There's a saying in Spanish, "El que paga, manda" –he who pays, commands– and it reflects the spirit of this third secret.

When you get a customer, you make a commitment. Not just the commitment to deliver, which you have to fulfill; you commit to care of their wellbeing. Yes, I know it is not legally your responsibility; we homo sapiens are predictably irrational, as Ariely says, and one of the irrational things we love is to be treated well.

And this is the foundation for my argument: being treated well does not mean cold, mechanical delivery of the service your customers purchased; it is all about making a difference giving the (real) impression that you care. That you care about their comfort; that you care about their benefit; that you care about their business, their personas, their world.

Sorry, people from other places; I am a Mexican, and one of our very positive traits is we are as nice as you can find, so listen to me. The third secret has this mandatory element, and I beg you to take my word when I tell you it works. If you are from a culture where relationships tend to be distant, cold and contact averse, don't worry. I'm not asking you to start hugging your customers; I'm asking you to treat them like royalty.

How?

Quite simple. We in Mexico are mocked by our Spanish Empire brothers for using the expression "*¿Mande usted?*" or, simpler, "*¿Mande?*". Well, don't listen to them, since evidence is our service is much better than theirs, and one of the reasons is we are educated to be at the service of others, and failing to do so will get us a sure reprimand from our elders –so, stick with us Mexicans on this one.

So, think of your attitude as "*¿Mande?*", or asking a real, committed, "What can I do for you?".

Yes. Ask "What can I do for you?" and then, do it.

Ask, then do.

Your customers will find it great when you ask about what can you do for them, and proceed to do it. It will be a huge differentiator from your competition, and will make you the leader on service –and operational complications.

So, let me give a little grain of salt for my advice. Us Mexicans, as kids, learned two things: to answer *¿Mande?*, and to negotiate after we got to know what our mothers wanted.

Lalito! Mande? I want you to go and buy some bread? Yes, Maam, and…?

Yes, and… that was the magic door to a place where the order would become a compromise of positions, giving something, getting something and, at the end, making both parties feel like they won something.

And that's the spirit behind "What can I do for you?"

People love to be pampered, yet our ancient culture is to make everybody subject to orders, conditions, limitations. Bureaucracy loves it; forbidding things, giving orders, saying things like "You have to…" is their day to day. Most customer service areas thrive with instructions, procedures, phrases such as "for your safety" or "do not". Lawyers love to write long, complicated contracts where all responsibility falls on the customer.

> *And yet we blame our customer loss on others.*
> *Such a pity.*

The third secret is aimed towards satisfaction. Customer satisfaction. Yes, I know there's no causal relation between it and loyalty; our goal is also to increase variables such as Net Promoter Score, which is an indicator of satisfaction if not loyalty.

Our goal, when we are in the quest for customer loyalty, is to achieve at least three things, remember? Increase customer retention, satisfaction, and average revenue per customer. So, the third secret aims towards customer satisfaction, and is supported by the "Yes, and..." tactic.

Yes, it is a tactic, and a powerful one, if you ask me. Is it easy to make a part of your company's culture? No. It is hard. It will take you at least a couple of years to see the results, and the rewards are beautiful indeed: Just imagine how your customers would feel if the answer to every question was "yes, ma'am, and..."; "yes, sir, and..."; "yes, customer, and..." followed by impeccable delivery.

Do you see it? Can you connect with your customers' feelings?

Let me propose a hypothetical situation. You are a hotel and one of your customers wants an upgrade on her room because [write your customer's reason here], and you don't have any available rooms. Standard procedure would be to answer a straight "No", in the most polite way, to continue with your important work, such as serving other customers.

But, and this is the important part, what if you answer "Yes, and I only have to wait for a room to be available. It might take even a couple of days and, if it happens, I will be delighted to give you what you ask for"... and you have your processes ready to support that offer?

One funny thing about the three secrets is they work better when they are used together. When I designed the COS Model, which is the model from where the three secrets come from, they were intended to be independent, so you could choose to use one, two or the three of them, whatever suited you. After a lot of analysis, I changed my mind.

When I was a kid, there was this saying in my Mom's family: *"con la boca que dije que sí, digo que no"* – with the mouth I said yes with, I say no – and it was a terrifying thing to hear. It meant, somehow, Mom, Grannie or Grandpa had made up their minds and changed their decisions.

Same thing happened to me after we implemented the model and started delivering workshops where we shared the three secrets: They work well together and, if you happen to let one of them out, you are missing the synergetic effect that make your customers strongly loyal to your brand. Would you like that to happen? Neither would I, so stay with me on this.

When you use the third secret, you are letting your customers know how valuable they are to you, and how you are willing to do something beyond your duty to treat them as royalty.

There's a catchy phrase, "exceed your customers' expectations". Everybody loves it and use it to fill their mouths with it... not me. I don't like it; I loath it. I despise it, because it is a piece of fake wisdom that only get us in trouble, since it is almost impossible to implement into your processes –and remember, I am a process guy too.

Let's say for the sake of argument, that you force me to accept it. Well, the third secret would be the perfect place for it. Yes, and… is a way to change your customers perception about you and how you satisfy their needs, it is an open answer, full of expectations, and a great way to tell your customer "Yes, I will work to exceed your expectations. If I do not have a clue about how to do it yet, I will do what I have to do to accomplish the task". And it may be well perceived as exceeding expectations, since the normal service we get from a brand is so dull, so empty, that making promises, even open ones, is a way to make the customer feel exceeded on expectations… provided that we will have the means to do something afterwards –and that's when secret number one comes into play, by the way.

See? The three secrets are easy to adopt, easy to implement, and hard to follow. Just like a lot of things in business life.

Have you read Amazon's history? Have you been a customer of Wynns, Starbucks, or Zappos'[3]?

Even when none of them started as a huge organization, the four companies knew what they wanted to accomplish. Customer loyalty, operational excellence and flawless customer communications. Neither Jeff Bezos, Howard Schultz, Tony Hsieh, nor Steve Wynn read my

---

[3] *The Everything Store*, or *Delivering Happiness* are great reads, and will give you great insights on companies who are famous for fulfilling their promises.

book –it wasn't out yet– and they had this clear understanding of what does it take to be number one:

> *Put in order the processes to do what you are telling your customer you will do… and do it right.*

> *Create the communication channels to be in touch with your customer, in a bidirectional manner… and do it right.*

> *Make your customer feel like royalty… and do it right.*

Amazon is a great example. It is focused on being the most customer centric company on earth, and everybody, from Jeff Bezos to the last clerk, works hard to achieve it.

Starbucks has over 28 thousand stores worldwide, and they have processes aimed towards making customers happy, like the one where they may offer coffee for free to customers who forgot their wallets –it may seem as a nicety, yet down under it is an operations decision: you can tell your customer to forget about the unpaid coffee, or you can give it away as a gift. On the first case, you get an angry customer and a wasted drink; on the second case, a happy customer and a coffee paid by your marketing budget. Which one do you prefer? See why I speak of processes that much? When properly stated, they are great tools.

If you are going to give a customer a free coffee, you better have the processes on place to make it happen without disrupting your financials, while at the same time presenting it as something you are proud to do for your valuable and loved customers –using the second secret, by the way.

The final effect is the same, you give a drink for free, so the second approach is much more beneficial for business than the first one. See?

Now that I made my point, let's go get the cook book to give you the recipe. You've got all the way here, you earned it.

Come with me. You'll be delighted.

. . . . .

TAKE AWAYS

Execute. Even if you are short on resources, execute.

The right offer, to the right customer, through the right channel, at the right time.

Processes are the secret for delivering standardized, good products and services time after time, and getting satisfied customers.

Make your customer feel like royalty.

The three strategies work better when used together. Don't leave anyone out.

The secret to great *Mole* is to know how.

> *Granma, how come everybody knows what mole has, and not all moles are the same?*
>
> *Because not everybody knows how to stir it, for how long, at what temperature, m'hijito.*

This is my recipe, and I will share it with you... only if you make a promise. (If you are not willing to do so, please close this book and resume your daily activities).

Ready? Repeat after me:

> *"I promise to use this knowledge for the good of my customers and my brand, to give it the best use possible, so my customer base remains loyal to us for many, many years".*

On behalf of your customers, thank you!

Before we begin, make sure you have two things regarding customer loyalty: The objectives and key results we discussed previously. What do you want to accomplish, and what will you measure to know if you are getting there.[4]

To move on, the first secret requires you to remember three things:

People. Processes. Technology.

---

[4] If you want to know more about OKRs, there's this very good article written by Falon Fatemi for Forbes, called "Want To Set Goals Like Google? Use OKRs".

Think of a triangle. Though there may be several types, they always have to have three sides. In our case, those three are people, or those guys who will be in charge of making things happen –yes, even in the digital world, there's people in several links of every value chain– and deliver your customers what you offered; processes, or the recipes to get things done in a consistent manner; and technology, or the tools and resources to make those processes a reality.

People are in charge of designing, building, implementing, managing, executing or controlling the way you deliver your offer. Processes are the "to do" lists. Technology is the machinery, the devices needed to deliver what people will do based on processes. See? The three sides are connected.

To begin, discuss people.

Let me ask you about some industries, either services or goods, and take a few moments to think about how people may get involved on those activities I just mentioned.

Ready? What about…

…hotels and hospitality?

　　…airlines?

　　　　…personal care?

　　　　　　…finance?

...consumer electronics?

...salt?

...pet food?

See?

People are at the core of all of them, either by clearly delivering, as in airlines or hotels and hospitality, or helping you decide which way to go with your money, as in finance.

The main problem is we, as organizations, have forgotten how important people are to achieve our goals, to fulfill our mission... the very mission we publish everywhere we can, and nobody gives a peanut about.

Regarding you as a manager, what's your job about people?

There's this hollow discussion about a leader and a manager, and I will not fall for it. Based on Peter Druker's vision, a manager has, among other duties, the role of forming and leading people towards the company's goals.

Remember the goals we set at the beginning of this section? They are three: Reduce customer turnover, increase satisfaction, and grow average revenue per customer.

What is our job relative to those goals and our people? Easy. Our job is to train, be an example, set goals, reward success, correct deviations, and, in extreme cases, let go.

Yes, if you are a manager, and above all, a customer oriented manager, you have to make sure your people are ready and prepared to face whatever challenges their customer pose, and do it in both a gallant and effective manner. Your job is to prepare your team with such weapons and skills as to take good care of business when it comes to serving your customers.

Above all, you have one job regarding your people: you have to make the "Yes, and…" culture be a part of all of your team's way of living.

What do I mean by this?

Companies have cultures, informal organization, rules and people relationships which transform into a way of life. Besides the formal life, where everything goes according to policies, strategies and plans, informal organization has strong power. It has been known for many, many years, in most cultures.

So, when I talk about making "Yes, and…" a part of your team's way of living, I am well aware about what I am talking.

Imagine the following: A customer calls your office and one finance guy picks up the phone. She is asking for help because her product is not doing what was expected.

She is a customer. She gives her money to your company for your products. What do you expect that finance guy to answer? –no, I'm not talking about what you assume will happen, I'm asking about what you expect.

Something nice, right? Not something from the finance department protocol, cold and number oriented; instead, say something heartfelt, warm, useful. Something like *"Yes, ma'am, and I will do this and that to help you"*.

That's my point. I am talking about having a company where everybody is aware of customers and how they are important to the organization's well being, so their answer to any contact, natural or accidental, has to come from their most natural attitude… and it happens when things are part of your way of life.

That's the people part. What about processes?

Processes are core to every periodical human activity. It doesn't matter if you prepare fried eggs for dinner (which, by the way, was the first process I ever diagrammed as an engineering student); you need to take into consideration three things: The input, the throughput, and the output.

Input is everything you need to perform the process. From raw materials to infrastructure to money, you need clarity on what you need to put **into** the process to get what you expect.

In my fried eggs example, input refers to eggs, olive oil, a pan, a working stove, salt, and chili pepper (sorry, it is my process, and I'm a hotchili-holic). Without any of these, the process won't deliver what I want.

Throughput refers to the process itself. What happens when, who is in charge, and how to be sure things don't collide with other things or activities.

Back to my fried eggs example, you have to turn on the stove, heat the pan, add some oil, wait a little, and crack open a couple eggs to put them on the pan together with salt and pepper. Add salt and chili pepper, wait for some time and, when the white is as white as you want it, take them off the pan and put them in a plate. By the way, if you realize I didn't mention the plate in the input section, it can become a problem; I didn't have a plate, now I have to get one or I will have no place to put my egg on.

Maybe you are thinking "What kind of dummy Lalo thinks I am?". No, I don't think you are a dummy, and we are not really talking about fried eggs, are we?

We are talking about making sure a customer oriented process works, and there's lots of things we may forget, much worse than a simple plate.

What if you decided to promise your customers a 72 hour delivery, and you forgot to ensure your vendors or logistics are up to the commitment? What if you get your product from China, and it takes the ship three months to get to you?

You'll have to make a decision, regarding your promise. Will you keep it or not? If you decide to keep it, you have to do something to correct the delay. Maybe using air freight, which will cost you several times more than a ship will do. Maybe going to your competition to purchase from them and deliver to your customer. Maybe, you will make no money and have a happy customer, nonetheless.

Leaving a step out of your process is much more damaging to business than forgetting a plate, so I am not a dummy, I was just trying to give you an easy example.

Review your processes. How many plates are you forgetting?

Let's go for the third side of our triangle. Technology. I love it. Technology is how we do things. They say scientists discover what is, and engineers create what isn't. Technology fascinates us since Archimedes wrote about the lever, Watt perfected the steam machine, or lasers became a part of our everyday language. We love technology; we love to use it and make our life easier in every sense.

In our understanding of what technology is, we can create devices, techniques, tools that don't exist, to accomplish our goals in an easier, faster, cheaper, manner. Our goal may be to fry a potato to give it the right crispiness, to get to the moon, or to send a picture to another person anywhere on earth. Technology does it for us, and we love it.

For some strange reason, technology is now associated with electronics, when it is a much broader concept. It may be quite basic, as the Archimedes lever, or a wheel to help us transport heavy loads for long distances, or a sophisticated device to look inside our brain in order to find out what is wrong with it. Technology is our way of being stronger, faster, or more accurate when we perform everyday tasks.

And that's what I talk about when I say technology. We have people ready to work, we have the processes on place; what we need now is the technology to step in.

What's the technology on my fried eggs example? Controlled high temperature. Devices to handle the eggs and let them cook without spilling around. Safety measures to avoid explosions. Devices to manipulate the product without burning our fingers... also known as stoves, turners and skillets.

Have you ever thought of a device where we can have high temperatures in a controlled manner, and use them without any risk to get burned and die? To use those high temperatures at will, and have them available whenever we need them, so we can process something for as long and warm as we need, without being subject to nature's caprice?

Well, a stove, and oven are such things. They are pieces of technology that can work with gas, coal, firewood or electricity, and still get us the same result: the perfect fried eggs, the perfect roast beef, or a warm cup of tea.

What do I mean about technology when I am talking about the triangle? Well, you defined a process, and you have people with "Yes, and..." as their way of living.

How do you make sure they are able to reach the levels you expect them to reach in a consistent manner?

With the proper technology, of course.

I'm not talking about high tech, just the necessary tech. And this is quite a subject in these times when companies fall for the misconception that apps –or applications– rule. No, apps are just tools to help us provide a service or getting in touch with customers (we'll discuss those when we get to the integrated communications strategy") and technology goes way farther than a simple app... so let me do a pit stop to discuss digital transformation.

Digital transformation is a buzz word which has many followers. A lot of companies are fighting to achieve it, many schools are devoting courses to it, and many professionals are specialized on it. What is it?

Let me give you my quick and dirty definition: Digital transformation is to move your organization from the physical world to the digital world. Simple, yet full of tricks. To move an organization to the digital world makes us think about many things –including the people-process-technology triangle– to ensure things work and you deliver your value proposition to your customers in both the digital and physical worlds.

It is a challenge. To move from physical to digital doesn't require you leave the physical way of doing things behind, just to take whatever fits your new condition and keep doing it, discarding what is useless, and creating new skills and abilities to serve your customers in the digital world. And as a good challenge, it forces you to think, and to think hard, so you can identify which parts of the process will change, and which will remain as they are. Remember the Blue Ocean strategy? Well, it has a lot to do with digital transformation: Raise things above, or lower things below your industry standards; create things your industry has never offered, or eliminate those your industry has always offered and you'd like to take away.

Based on this, let's assume you have a pizza franchise, and want to transform it for the digital world. What would change in your business model and your value proposition? Your sales channels? Your payment methods? Your purchasing? Just think the Blue Ocean way...

What about your delivery? Would you go digital? How? How can you digitalize the delivery process? The production process? Will you get robots? Drones? Guys on bikes?

The digital transformation of your processes is a huge task, and it may be endless if you have the vision and a huge budget. As regular organizations often do, you have limited resources and need to make decisions based on that fact, so, let me ask again: How far would you go to transform your organization?

The answer you give me has to become your reference. If you say "I'll do as little as necessary", it means you will be making your decisions based on economy and spending as little as possible. If you say "whatever it costs", then you are set for an adventure on digitalization. At the end, is there a right answer?

No, and don't let the voices out there fool you. There's not a minimum level of digital transformation. Nor there's a general objective when doing it. Digital transformation is like interior design: you decide what suits you, and then you go for it.

So, how much technology would you apply to your pizza franchise? According to my proposal, it depends on your vision and budget. Nobody else's.

Assuming you already decided what level you need to deliver the offer you made to your customers, and what type of technology you need to achieve it, go for it. Make a decision and get the technology you deem necessary. Ah, and don't listen to others.

Everybody has a word on technology. Somehow processes get more respect, since they are kids of mental work; technology is often subject to "have you heard how they are doing it over at…".

Don't listen to them. Just don't.

You are in charge of your decisions, and as so you have to have a healthy level of stubbornness. Believe in your self and your ability to make decisions. If you start listening to others, you will have a mess –while you will still be the accountable one. Imagine Ford, or Jobs, or Bezos, falling for what others think is better? Me neither, so be stubborn and keep your decisions dear to your heart.

People, processes and technology. Check!

TAKE AWAYS

The goal is to satisfy customers in a consistent manner.

Digital transformation is to move your organization from the physical world to the digital world.

Technology is only as good as you are using it; not the other way around.

When it comes to technology, don't listen to others. Don't.

Who's gonna do it? How?

Maybe my team had not the best and brightest, but we were the most motivated, most prepared, best equipped team possible.

Together, we beat our competition –it was the greatest of joys.

We've discussed just a little the three elements of my loyalty operations triangle (well, even when it is not my creation, I love it and like to call it mine; I hope you do it too, soon). Let me go over them in more detail.

People.

People are in charge of designing, building, implementing, managing, executing or controlling the way you deliver your offer. It includes those guys working to deliver the service or product, those who manage the business, those who do indirect tasks such as accounts receivable or human resources, and all of them are people.

Processes are how we will accomplish that task, in a repeated, trustable manner. They describe how things flow, what is done when, by whom, where do activities start and stop, so they can be repeated time after time, applying the necessary controls when needed, so everything is delivered in the most uniform way, with consistent quality.

Technology is what will help us maintain the processes operating and reaching the levels we ask from them. It is more than electronics or digital; it is the application of scientific knowledge to reach our goals. A press, a stove, a laser, a rocket, all of them are technology, and in each case we reach some goal: A printed book, a cooked meal, an eye surgery, or a space trip.

So, what to do with each to reach what we expect on the operational side? Simple. Let's begin with people and what the model requires them to do.

There's three things about people that the model needs: attitude, skills and tools.

The first thing you want to work on is attitude, since it is part of culture and takes a lot of time to sink in. The route I like most begins with Customer Orientation and "Yes, and…". It means you have to get your people through a path of training, discussion, divulgation, where they get to understand the customers, the reasons they purchase from the company, the motivations they have to stay or to leave, the standards they measure the company's performance by, their unsatisfied needs, desires and wants, etc.

So, take some time to schedule three seminars with all your people; if they are in multiple locations, prepare the dates and places so you can deliver the seminar throughout the different locations in no more than a month per subject, so you cant take six to eight months to finish the rollout.

The model recommends you go for three things: Customer Insight, Customer Oriented Behavior, and Customer Protection.

Customer Insight.

Insights are motivations, reasons why people act, so they get rid of pains, they get benefits or they simplify their day-to-day activities. They are not data, nor needs, nor common truths. Insights are deep understandings of your customers reasons to act, and they are very pleasurable to understand, since it is much better to understand that a housewife purchases from you because she wants to feel successful thru her family's successes after she sends them with their flashing white clothes to school and work and they get compliments for that, so she feels she is doing a great work doing her job… than to understand that 67.8% of stay-at-home mothers want a more effective detergent.

One great way for your employees to get those insights is via direct interaction. Consider bringing a customer to talk to them in a panel or an interview. If they can't, ask for a recorded interview that you can edit and project later at the seminars. If those are not options, then send somebody to have a depth interview with them –nobody from the team who serves that customer, by the way; they try to embellish reality, and even give their own perception about the customer's answers. Send somebody who doesn't know the customer that well, with a well prepared interview guide, so they know what to ask for.

Customer Insights give everybody, with direct and indirect relationships with customers, fresh views on what they think they provide, and what customers expect from the firm. It may even be a bittersweet experience, worth the time for everyone, you'll see.

The Customers Insights seminars have one simple goal, to let **everybody** know what the customers expect from the company, so they may serve them better.

> Fulfilling their insights is the reason why your customers buy from you… unfulfilling them is the reason why your ex-customers are no longer with you.

Get it?

With the Customer Insights seminar you just put everybody on customer mode. There is no further excuse to say things such as "This is what customers expect from us" without any support. Nobody is allowed to say "I know these customers like anybody else" without sharing the insights they have about such customers… what their pains are, what benefits do they expect, which jobs and tasks are they expecting to simplify or eliminate.

Customer Oriented Behavior.

Once everybody is in customer insight mode, you have to go for the behavior. It is easier to change an attitude about your customers when you know and understand them. To change your company's customer culture, the first step is putting everybody on their side, and then come with some recipes on how to behave –remember how your family educated you? Think about it. Families have traditions, ways of doing things –I am writing this on Christmas day; last night we had the *Arrullo*, which is a Mexican tradition to celebrate the birth of Baby Jesus. The songs we sing, the prayers we say, the candles we light, all come from late 19th century, and all of us Araujos have been educated on them, year after year, Christmas Eve after Christmas Eve, generation after generation.

Why the *Arrullo* example? Because it is the same with companies. You have to have a culture, traditions, stories; you have to tell everybody what the important things are, so they may act accordingly.

How? The first thing you have to do –and it was the reason why you collected insights– is the foundation for your culture. Customers are important resources for your company, and understanding them is a way to feel a part of something bigger than a day-to-day job.

The second thing is to go for the Customer Oriented Behavior seminar. Just as you did with Customer Insights, schedule a one day seminar to go over four things from your company's Business Model: the Value Proposition, the interaction Channels and the Customer Relationships you are after, and the Revenue Streams.

Everybody in direct and indirect customer contact positions, has (I repeat) has to understand these four elements, so they make the link between the insights and how the company satisfies them[5].

Next item on the agenda is "Yes, and…". Why? Because it opens the door to further negotiations, new business and opportunities. When customers ask for something, and they get a "Yes" for an answer, they open their minds while giving room for going into deeper understanding to support action, modify it or even deny it, with a positive attitude.

How?

Simple. Yes, and… leaves a sliver for modifying things. It is not a final answer. The "and…" component lets you add anything you need to provide what your customer is asking for, always on a positive way.

Let me give an example. You are the engineering chief of a logistics company, and one mid value customer comes with a weird request: She wants her merchandise to be transported in red containers, painted Pantone Red-032-C – your company corporate color is yellow. What would you answer, yes or no?

To say yes means you are agreeing to her request with no hesitations, and you are in trouble.

To say no means to annoy the customer, and you are in trouble.

---

[5] It is not optional. Everybody is in direct or indirect contact with customers has to understand those four elements.

To say "Yes, and I have to check under which conditions we may provide it", opens a huge, huge door. Do you see it?

It opens the door to growing the business with this particular client; it opens the door to negotiation, it opens the door to a price increase, because you take the ball to your court, and now she is expecting the conditions under which her request will work.

I love answering "Yes, and..." and I learnt it the hard way. I had this customer for whom we designed and built a statuesque symbol, and he later asked us to move it to a risky position. Instead of opening a door, I opposed, since my customer's best interest was on my mind, and risking the statue would be unacceptable... something else was on **his** mind, and he found a way to do it, paying for it, **with another company**. It was one of the hardest lessons I got on customer oriented behavior. Customers want solutions, not reasons why not. If you open the door for thinking, you can even make it together and charge for it; if you close the door, he will do it, even without you... and you don't want to lose that revenue, do you?

Yes, and...

This is the right answer to let your customers know you care about them, you want to do whatever they are looking for, and give you room to come up with a win-win proposal.

Second part of Customer Oriented behavior is to let everybody in the organization understand how a company lives from the money their customers pay for goods and services. Yes, it is the moment to review such concepts as profit and loss, costs, expenses and profit, regardless of their positions and expertise, so there's no doubt where money comes from and where does it go.

You don't have to disclose sensitive information; you can just relativize it: You can say how, from each $100 your company gets, $39 go to costs, $47 to expenses and the remaining $14 are pretax profit.

My approach is simple; first, I give the rough numbers on revenue, costs and expenses, then I talk about the three segments: Most important customers, important customers and regular customers. What do I mean by that?

This: How much of those profits and revenue come from each type of customer, and how many of them are there in each segment. This clarifies a lot of things. Instead of saying things such as "They are important because they've been with us for many years", or other qualitative argument, you switch to "Those customers are important because 29% of our profit and 32% of our revenue come from them". Draw a graph and put together three variables in it: How many customers are in each segment, how much revenue they generate, and how much profit comes from that revenue. Do it and you'll see how much your people's attitude changes, since they get two messages: We perceive you as responsible professionals, and this is the consequence of loosing one customer from each segment.

> *Let your people understand how valuable your customers are, so they understand the impact of loosing one to the competition.*

See? Your people need to be informed on your customers' value and importance to the organization. Each member of your team has to be aware of how much is at stake if a customer is lost, and why you keep talking about very important, important, and regular customers; and acquisition, retention and growth strategies are not only buzz words; they are vital roads to maintain your customer base alive and well.

Customer Oriented Behavior is a way of living if you want to have loyal customers, to retain them, to grow the business with them, and to get new customers because of recommendations. That's why it is the second element: First, you have to understand your customers and their motivations; second, everybody in the organization has to act with them in mind; third, you need to give your people the tools to protect the customers.

Customer Protection.

It's time for the operational phase. You just gave your people the tools to understand your customers and treat them based on their needs, wants and desires.

Now, it is time to build up the defense system. I don't know how much more expensive it is to get a new customer versus keeping one. According to my experience, it's not an easy task to get new customers; on the contrary, it is hard as nails to go out there and get somebody to believe your value proposition is so valuable as to give you their money... that's why so many people are afraid of sales –I know, I've led sales forces, and good salespeople are quite a challenge to find.

So, what is my proposal? Simple. Everybody in the organization must feel responsible of keeping customers. There's nobody whose job is not to keep customers satisfied. Nobody. It is quite the opposite, and let me state it as a law. Let's call it the First Law of Customer Conservation:

It is everybody's job to keep customers.

From the most experienced executive, to the freshmen in the on-boarding process, all people in the organization have the job of keeping customers. It means you have to give people the tools, skills, and indicators to do it.

Quantitative tools. Decision making capabilities. Objective means to know what is going on and make a decision so the First Law of Customer Conservation is enforced.

Skills. Customer service skills. The skills to make decisions to give customers the best, even if they go against traditional company policies. The skills to use the company resources in order to fulfill customers' requests. I don't know how many types of skills you'll have to train your people on; these two are a good starting point.

...And indicators. Life without indicators would be miserable for our people when dealing with customers. Indicators are numbers that let people know if things are going according to plan. They are objective tools for making informed decisions, and you need your people to do so, if you want to have a mature organization that manages its customers' loyalty.

There's three general indicators that you have to use per segment: Net Promoter Score (NPS); average revenue per customer; and customer retention index. Everybody has to know where these indicators are, and know the trend from period to period.

Also, each customer has to be part of a group. Everybody has to know if a particular customer is a member of the very important, important, or regular customer group. Yes, you may name those groups as you want, and it is mandatory that everybody in the organization knows what does each customer group mean.

Regarding which customers are in each group, I have a rule of thumb: The more important the customers are, the more necessary it is they know it, and the name of their group. Why? Because for them it is a matter of pride, and forces you to be swift and accurate when you have to serve them or make a decision about their relationship with your firm.

Do lesser value customers have to know how much they mean to the firm? No, but this is the reason why the even ground rule exists: All your customers have an even ground, with the same basic rights; they will get what your value proposition establishes, regardless of their value to the company.

The even ground rule spirit is simple: Nobody gets bad service. Nobody receives lesser quality. Nobody is below what your value proposition says. Is there an exception? Yes, the very important and important customers –they are above your value proposition and are subject to better service, better quality, an improved value proposition.

That approach is the difference between a customer loyalty oriented organization and the rest. Let's call it the Second Law of Customer Conservation:

Each and every customer get what your business model promises, with no excuses.

It is a simple statement, yet a powerful commitment. If you want loyal customers, you have to abide by these laws. And by you, I mean everybody in your organization. Period.

How can we ensure great service? That's a job for the second dimension of the loyalty operations triangle: Processes.

Processes.

A process is a structured approach to achieve a goal in a repeated manner. They have a stigma, nonetheless, as a part of hard operations, manufacturing or complex activities. Truth be told, every customer related activity has a process behind, even an informal one.

Think about companies such as Disney, McDonalds, Starbucks, Zappos, or Southwest. There are processes everywhere, and that's how they make sure they provide the same service, with the same quality, to each of their customers, always –and they serve them by millions per year.

Have I told you I'm an industrial engineer? Well, I am, and one of the things I love about my career is the obsession with measuring, timing, charting, sequencing, in order to standardize activities and make sure they are optimized and repeatable.

Well, from now on, you have to be an industrial engineer at heart. You will work on decomposing your service into tiny elements, into steps, decisions, input and output, so you make sure your throughput is such that your customers will always get what you promised them. Always.

I already told you about *The Founder*, the story of Ray Kroc and McDonalds; it has very important lessons. One of them is when he gets into a fight with his franchisees because they are selling chicken and other things, breaking the restaurant's value proposition. The other one is how much he emphasized standardization; he was obsessed with it , and it proved to be the right obsession. If you want to grow and keep things under control and standardize your products or services, your process will need three things: Standard inputs; standard throughput, and standard output (yes, is what Elijahu Goldratt proposed in *The Goal*).

Is your inner industrial engineer ready? Gather a team of people who understand what the company does to deliver the value proposition, and chart it. Make sure you identify who is in charge of what, when does it have to happen, what the inputs and previous steps are, and what the results have to be. Put all of that in writing. Times, places, people in charge. Be sure you chart all of it.

Is there a mandatory form of doing it? No. You may use a Gantt chart; an algorithm; a flow chart; anything goes if you feel comfortable with it and how it represents the process.

I, myself, like to use flow charts. I like them, and develop them in two steps. First, I write down the steps, as a simple algorithm, and review it to be sure we have everything written down. Then, I draw the flow chart, and review it under two conditions: With the team who drew it, and on the field, where the real action is. This second part is better done with somebody from outside the team, a person who is not biased by your thoughts or thoughts about a particular item, so the process is reviewed by what it describes, not what it should describe.

Another tool I love is mental maps. They are representations of reality made with diagrams, figures, drawings, relationships, arrows, and whatever goes to describe your idea –your process, in this case. Even though a mental map is not as formal as a flow chart, it does the job in a joyful manner. Use them if you want to keep formality down, while not loosing effectiveness.

At this point, you may be asking yourself "what's the relationship between a process and the Laws of Customer Conservation?" Simple.

The first law says it is everybody's job to keep customers. The second law says each and every customer get what your business model promises, with no excuses. To take it beyond written letter and turn it into action, you have to create the processes to ensure it happens.

Let me give an example. Have you ever been to Starbucks? Have you ever said your drink is not what you were expecting? Their promise is your drink will be perfect every time, and they have the processes in place to make it happen. Without asking any questions, they will prepare you a drink again, until you are satisfied. If it looks simple, just think about the implications: There's raw materials to create every drink, and they all cost. How are they accounted for? There's no revenue for the new drink; how do you absorb the cost for the materials? There's other people in line, who also have to be served. How do you serve one person more than once?

All of the answers to those questions are in processes. Accounting for the cost of raw materials; defining a budget for those expenses; training your baristas so they are able to take care of new orders while correcting defective ones. Yes, I am a regular Starbucks customer, and every time I see that happening I get a sense of awe. They are focused on satisfying their customers, and instead of fighting for the petty costs of a new Decaf Frappuccino Low Fat Extra Milk No Foam, they focus on getting it right, knowing that the extra cost is a marketing expense, instead of a spoiled drink.

On the other hand, think of those many vendors you buy from, guys who refuse as hard as they can to go the extra mile to keep you satisfied. How do you feel? Are you a happy customer? Do you like the feeling of giving them your hard earned money? How open are you to take a new option, buying for a lower price or better service?

Well, those same thoughts go through your customers' minds... and they are not nice.

I am not suggesting that you throw everything away and start charting processes as crazy. No. Quite the opposite. I want you to start on a simple manner. Identify the two or three most important processes to deliver your value proposition, and go for them. I am aware that you are in charge of loyalty on a living organization, and things have to keep up and running. So, my proposal is this: Go and find the three processes your value proposition is more dependent on, chart them and make sure those in charge of executing them understand and know them by heart, so they execute impeccably. I call it the Third Law of Customer Conservation:

People have to understand and know the processes by heart, and execute them impeccably.

What do I mean by this?

I am not talking about perfection. I am talking about performing at the top of your class. I am talking about doing things right, at the first try, always... and if you do not, have the means to insure it is corrected and your customers receives what they pay for, in the less stressful manner.

When your people understand the processes and what are they in charge of, to be impeccable is much easier. Let's say you manage a slow pizza place, and all of your employees do whatever they think is needed to deliver a slow pizza, when they think it's right. Imagine the mess?

On the other hand, think you have all the processes in place, and each and every member of your team knows what they do and when, subject to a delivery time between 60 and 75 minutes, in such conditions that your customers get a warm, traditional pizza, with the ingredients they asked for. Do yo see the difference?

Good processes and impeccable execution are at the core of every successful company. Think of those brands you are most loyal to. How do they execute? How do they treat you every time you purchase from them? Is the experience something you look forward for, or just a jackin-the-box-like experience, where you know you will be surprised with random quality services or products?

Let me tell you a little secret: Processes are the most important part for conquering your customers' loyalty. Customers have expectations, and your job is to satisfy them. To deliver in such manner that those expectations are regularly met, creating a sense of trust in your customers, so that they know you deliver… and that, my friends, is the very foundation of loyalty.

> ***Consistent, repeated satisfaction of customers' expectation, is the very foundation of customer loyalty.***

What I am talking about is as old as business. Since that time when smiths started working in the same streets back in the middle ages, they had to compete for getting and retaining customers. And that's how brands came by. They were the means each smith used to differentiate their work from the guy next door's. And it implied a lot of things, like quality, service, durability, and satisfaction of expectations.

Imagine you are a farmer back in 13th century, and need a new plow for this season. Who'd you go to? The blacksmith who delivered late four years ago, or his neighbor who has always been there whenever your horses need new horseshoes?

That, my friends, is the spirit behind this book. If you make a promise, deliver. If you tell your customers you will do something for them, do it. If you have a value proposition, be sure you have the processes in place to deliver it every single time.

Remember the expression "a man of his word"? Well, your organization has to be "a firm of her word". You have to deliver always, in a consistent manner, to meet your customers expectations about their needs, desires or wants. If you want to exceed them, it's up to you, just remember you will also have to design a way to do it consistently, according to the rules and decisions to do it, since once you exceed expectations, your customer will see that as your baseline, and you have to deliver up to that new level now and always.

> ***Once you exceed expectations, your customer will get used to that, and you'll have to deliver again and again and again… improving every time.***

Take a minute or two to chart one of your processes. Bring a sheet of paper –digital or physical, it doesn't matter– where you may start using three archetypical figures: Rectangles for activities, rhombuses for decisions and questions, circles for connections. Leave the other figures for later.

Ready? Select a simple process around your value proposition, and start drawing it like a flowchart, using vertical lines to divide what one area or person does, before responsibility goes to the next one.

What did you get? Is it clear? Do you feel confident on how it represents the way your value proposition is supposed to be delivered?

Now, take a little bit longer and get out of the building, to talk with one or two customers. Do they think the process you charted will deliver what they expect from you? If it does, congratulations! You just stated a process in a clear manner; if not, go back, redo the chart, and repeat your contact with customers until you get an affirmative answer. Then, get your people to know it by heart and perform it every time in an impeccable way.

Yes, I know I am quite pushy on the importance of processes and how to make them a fundamental element of your company's reflexes; it is my job to help you master how to get and manage your customers' loyalty... so please, when it comes to defining and documenting processes, do as I ask you. Think of me as a coach.

What if you don't document your processes? Havoc. No, I am not joking. Without documented processes you get great confusion and disorder, and that's the very definition of havoc.

Remember *The Founder*? Well, back in the 90's, when I was an MBA student, the term *McDonaldization* was created by George Ritzer, and I remember four elements as key for it: Efficiency, Calculability, Predictability and Control.

If you standardize your processes with these four elements, you are ready to deliver what you offer in a consistent manner, which is what your customers expect.

Am I advocating a return to 20th century? Not at all; I'm just putting on the table some of the basic concepts for delivering homogenous quality. Just like beauty, value is in the eye of the beholder but... we have to make sure we produce services, products and experiences that are the same, that feel the same, regardless of time, place and who is in charge.

Imagine you are the in charge of operations at Chez Gustave, a French restaurant with very loyal customers, and one of your main dishes are *Escargot à la Provence*. Your secret recipe has been the best kept secret since Gustave's beloved grand mother passed it to him when he was just a little boy, many years ago. She even wrote it down herself:

Escargot à la Provence.

...par Granmère.

300 g fresh butter	1. Leave the butter soften at room temperature; add the echalottes, chopped garlic, chopped parsley (save some for later), Pernot, white wine and french herbs.
25 g echalottes	
50 g garlic (chopped)	
50 g parsley (chopped)	
20 ml Pernot	
35 ml white wine	2. Season with Worcestershire sauce, Maggi seasoner, salt and white pepper. Mix.
¼ teaspoon herbs de Provence	
Worcestershire sauce	
Maggi seasoning juice	3. Put some seasoned butter in each shell, add the escargot and top with some more seasoned butter.
Salt	
White pepper	
15 g chopped bre crums	
24 escargots	4. Cook in the oven for 10-15 minutes at 200°C, until butter turns gold.
24 shells	
	5. Serve with bread crumbs and chopped parsley.

Imagine your place is famous for this recipe –remember, a recipe is also a process– and your strategic plan is to expand nationally, opening your first branch in another city, with other people in charge of cooking it, and other vendors.

As I said, this is your signature dish; how much are you willing to risk if it is not exactly the same in your new place? Would you take a chance for disappointing customers who already love your famous escargots, if they go to the new place and find they are prepared with onion instead of garlic, celery instead of parsley, and cognac instead of white wine?

Maybe this new recipe is good; maybe it is better that your original one. What if it is not as good, since it is not your signature recipe? Would you take the risk?

Let's propose a different scenario.

You bring your new cooks to your original place, teach them the recipe, and train them until they know the recipe by heart, until they can prepare dish after dish of those great escargots, and your loyal customers can't find the difference.

Then, once they are running the operation in your new place, you make surprise runs to ask for the escargots, and if you find they aren't as good as they should be, you reinforce your cooks' training, until they are back in track.

Those two scenarios are different, yet valid. Which one do you prefer?

The strategies this book talks about have no option. You have to go for the second scenario. You document your processes, you train your people on them, and you make sure they follow them –you don't punish, you control by reinforcing their skills until your people are back on the quality level your customer expects.

This is what organizations such as McDonalds and Starbucks do. They don't take the risks of delivering uneven quality on different stores, and they have the processes to ensure that quality. Just imagine! A process to be sure all your processes run smoothly... it is the ultimate way to know you will deliver what you promised, always.

Have you been a to a Starbucks abroad, let's say in Peru? To a McDonalds in Thailand?

Products and services quality are uniform, even though those countries may have cultural oddities. If you are in charge, will you take the risk of being like that Mexican airline known as Aeromaybe, whose service was everything except uniform... or a Starbucks, a McDonalds?

Me, I would much rather be one of the latter. I'd love my customers trusting in my brand everywhere they find it, regardless of the place or time they come in to purchase. What about you?

Yes, I've been incisive. I've been pushy. I've even used an escargot recipe to make my point – it is real, by the way; you can try it. Yet I do it all for a good cause: You will never regret being sure if your processes are well documented and followed by your people... your customers will notice it and your products and services will satisfy them each and every time they come to you.

Isn't that the goal?

Customers are a company most valued treasure; all revenue comes from their pockets, and there's no substitute for them. The three elements we just discussed have one objective: to keep your customers satisfied in such manner they don't look for other options.

Yes, we are homo sapiens, and so are your customers. They are predictably irrational, and some of them will leave no matter what, for reasons you may find impossible to understand. Yes, I am aware of it and the idea still stands: It is your job to minimize risk of loosing your customers, and to keep them so satisfied the number of those looking for another vendor is minimal. And those customers who resist the temptation to leave, buying your products or services with a good attitude towards you, those customers are loyal, my friends...

...and this book is all about customer loyalty, remember?

TAKE AWAYS

If you make a promise, deliver.

Once you exceed expectations, your customer will get used to it, and expect it every time.

Laws of customer conservation:

1. It is everybody's job to keep customers.

2. Each and every customer get what your business model promises, with no excuses.

3. People have to understand and know the processes by heart, and execute them impeccably.

Enough talk. Now, let's do it.

Who's gonna do it?

You are.

When I was a kid, I loved westerns. Those movies where a lonely cowboy, riding his horse through the western plains, was able to defeat everybody with just a .45 Colt revolver, fighting without loosing his hat, and having time to calm his thirst in a saloon with a shot of whiskey.

Oh, those guys who could save the whole town all by themselves...

Well, it is not like that anymore. To achieve his dream today, the cowboy would need a team, organization, tools and weapons. In modern days, those loners wouldn't get too far.

Imagine Mary Kay. She was a housewife, back in the days when married women had not many options; somehow she faced the challenge to make her own living, and she created Mary Kay Cosmetics, a company whose business model depends on people and their abilities to deliver demonstrations which lead to sales.

Would've been sufficient if Mary, all by herself, did it? Maybe, if you think on her survival only; to be a huge success, you have to have an organized team, with the tools and skills to do their job and provide their grain of sugar to the team's pile[6].

So, let's go to the *how to* section of this book.

How to implement the three strategies in your organization.

I've been discussing the whys and whats of customer loyalty, and the strategies to reach it. Now, let's talk about operations, activities, budget, and metrics.

Strategy	Tactics	Target	Leader	Three year budget
Integrated Communications	Hubert Direct	Customers	GR	$10,000
	Hubert Red Phone customers	Red Phone customers	AH	$25,000
		Red Phone customers	AH	$80,000
Customer orientation	Internal communications	Hubert México personnel	JB	$12,000
	Two-way internal communications	Hubert México personnel	SR	$37,200
	New service launch	Customers.	FB	$30,000
	Hubert, half a century	Customers.	ED	$60,000
Impecable Offering	Installation excellence	Supervisors; technicians and installation managers. Contractors.	FS	$16,000
	Hubert delivers	Hubert people related to fulfilling promises. Hubert customers.	FS	$25,000
	Maintenance excellence	Hubert personnel and customers	RE	$15,000
Total:				$310,200

---

[6] This is a metaphor my dear friend Octavio Herrero gave me once: Companies are like ants, who are building up this pile of sugar. To turn it into a gigantic pile, they need everybody, including employees and vendors, bringing even a single grain of sugar. Only after the pile is ready, solid, big, they will give each one its part.

I love it.

This is an example cover of a three year plan. Why that much? Because customer loyalty is not something to achieve overnight, and your organization has to be ready to make it part of its essence –*it's in our DNA*, as business people love to say.

If you do not know where you want to go, just don't go.

Remember your objectives, which I recommend to be expressed on three variables: Customer retention rate, Net Promoter Score (NPS), and average revenue per customer (ARPC)?

For the purposes of this chapter, you are the CEO of Loyalis:

> It serves over 14,600 customers per month, in twelve locations throughout the country, plus internet, and app, and a call center.
>
> Current NPS is 48, and has been stable for three years. It is measured quarterly by a third party.
>
> ARPC is $39.22, declining at a 2.4% yearly rate for the past five years. Your goal is to get it up to $47.67
>
> Customer retention rate is 89%, down seven points from two years ago, four points from last year.

Since you are the CEO, your board of directors is beginning to make questions, and some of them are uneasy about where you are taking the company. So, you ask yourself a question:

How can I improve these numbers?

Do not worry. The three strategies are the right tool for it. And you just have to put them into play with a simple plan.

First, do what traditional planning taught you. Define an objective for each variable. Where do you want to take them? Let me propose these:

Variable	Current value	End of year 3 objective	Gap
NPS	48	55	7
ARPC	$39.22	$46.67	$7.45
CRR	89%	92.50%	3.5pp

Are you satisfied? The three strategies take advantage of Drucker's good ol'management by objectives concept, and we will set FAST objectives. It means they will be:

Frequently discussed to monitor progress, allocate resources, prioritize initiatives, and exert control.

Ambitious, difficult –not impossible.

Specific. Clear. Related to measurable things, commonly understood, with no confusion.

Transparent. Yes, they must let everybody see what they are about, and understand it.

Yes, I am not a fan of SMART objectives. I'd rather go for FAST, and the three strategies assume you are too. Why?

Because you want everybody to get excited on how the team is advancing, how challenging the goals are, and how easy they are for all the team to understand them. When talking about customers and loyalty, you want all of your team members running in the same direction, at the same speed, with the same motivation.

Get the point?

Now, with those three FAST objectives, you are ready to do that thing they pay you so handsomely to do: Think.

There's this set of rules I manage my professional life by. Number nine is great: *When in doubt, think!* So, let's go and use rule #9. Let's think.

Take your team for a walk, to have a cup of coffee, host a design thinking session, or just draw an Ishikawa diagram. The means is not that critical, as much as you lead them to do one thing: Make them think on tactics to achieve those goals over a three year period.

Let them be creative. Let them be innovative. Let them be ambitious. Let them own the problem and the solution. Let them see Loyalis under new perspectives, so they can think on the new, customer-oriented Loyalis looks like.

Once you let your team work on the means, the tactics, the operations, what do you get? Lots of good things to implement over the years, in order to achieve the three objectives. (Yes, I refer to goals and objectives in an indistinct manner; when I have objective and subjective things in place, such as perception and revenue, I like to mix both concepts, to leave definition issues out of scope).

As I was saying, we have three objectives to achieve. This is the list of what your team proposed after that walk:

Send a newsletter to all customers talking about the new offers Loyalis has.

Create the role of Customer Officer, to give your customers an internal advocate who oversees their needs and helps them solve the many issues dealing with Loyalis has for them.

Assign a budget for corrections and defects solution; it will come from both your marketing and production indirect expenses, mainly people and training.

Train all your employees on Service Quality, so they know how to treat every single customer.

Send a note to all Loyalis employees letting them now the new objectives.

Deliver a seminar for all employees where they will learn about customer centricity and will sign a poster to show their commitment.

> *Write a set of quality guidelines and have attendees repeat them by heart, at the beginning of every meeting.*
>
> *Write down THE quality policy, print it on huge posters, and post it at the lobby on each and every office.*
>
> *Implement Net Promoter Score; measure it each quarter.*
>
> *Hire a quality coach, to work with employees every other week on subjects such as Ishikawa diagrams, histograms, and quality reports.*
>
> *Copy Wynns' program of great things done for customers, to put up on the internet those who do great things.*

Do you think it'll work?

I don't. Why?

Because they are a set of good, unrelated ideas, with no execution plan, no dates, no owners, no expected outcomes, no control metrics. And that's why so many loyalty efforts die young: Because they are sentenced to death before they are even born.

On the other hand, what happens if you put together a SWAT team, a thinking team, and give them the task to put together a plan, with no more than five actions per year, to accomplish your loyalty goals?

That's the purpose of the COS Model where the three strategies come from –we discussed it early on this book: Communications, Operations, Service; remember?

Forget Robin Hood's Merry Men style[7], and go for the professional, long term, business oriented approach.

Cut to the chase, and see what a think tank would deliver:

- Establish some goals to know where the company goes: i) increase average revenue per customer by 7% per year; ii) increase customer retention rate by 2 percent points per year; iii) grow NPS by 10 points per year
- Adopt three strategies for the next five years, so the company makes decisions with a clear view of what is to be done: Impeccable offering; integrated marketing communications; customer focus.
- Define a clear value proposition to let each employee understand what is it that customers expect from them and the company: *You will be served in the fastest and most convenient way.*
- Land one strategy at a time. On the first quarter, define three to five tactics for impeccable offer; then, on second quarter, those corresponding to customer orientation; then, integrated communications on year two, once the other two are up and running.
- Implement the tactics for each strategy, with their corresponding metrics.
- Assign an objective budget. (I like to go for the "What we need to do" budgeting approach. It means you quantify what you have to hire, purchase, develop, design, and add up a budget. Even better, if you have to

---

[7] It is the approach Robin Hood's mates would take to a particular task; neither strategic nor long term. Very tactical, effective on the short run, just to get away with their plan and annoy the Sheriff and get the money. The total opposite to the three strategies and COS Model.

negotiate and compromise it, you get an advantage: Each dollar you cut, is something you will have to take out, impacting expected outcome. That's a better position than saying "this is what the industry does", or "we made a benchmark and found that...". Believe me, it is a much better way to get a budget).

- Define a leader for each tactic. Nothing will happen if nobody's assigned as leader and has the accountability to deliver. Name one person per tactic, with the skills and intelligence to deliver; then, let them do their jobs. Do not micromanage. Do not.
- Go. Too much preparation kills great customer-oriented projects; go back to the skills I asked you about people on item seven. Get them. Let them work, and correct only if and when needed.
- One more thing: Let everybody in the organization know the objectives. Make them FAST.

See the difference? At the end, you will have a clear, visual means to communicate strategies, tactics, budget, metrics, and owners. That way there will be no need to look for someone to offer as sacrifice to the gods of business.

As one friend told me, easy is different from simple. Golf is a simple game where you hit a ball with a stick, to get it into a hole. Not easy at all... and I remember him with joy every time I hit the ball, by the way.

Getting your customers' loyalty is a simple game, yet it can be hard not to get lost in attractive formulas that take you nowhere, and just fill you with frustration.

Remember the goals we set for Loyalis? How focused do you think the organization will be on achieving them, once all employees know what is to be done, why, when, by whom, and how will the results be measured? In my experience, it goes hand in hand with execution –with *impeccable* execution– where everybody is well aware of what the final destination is, and how the trip is going, to make the necessary arrangements if the compass is lost, to go back in route as fast as possible.

So, let me ask again. How comfortable are you, as the top manager at Loyalis, that your company will achieve your customer related goals?

If I were you, I'd be quite comfortable, for sure. Why? Because Loyalis has a clear plan, from goals and strategies to tactics, budget and control metrics, with people in charge. It is just a matter of using your business acumen to put them to work and reach your objectives.

Disclaimer: Ever since I discovered them in college, I've been a true fan of strategic planning and the management process, so it's no wonder I root so hard for them.

· · · · ·

TAKE AWAYS.

Set FAST goals. Frequently discussed, ambitious, specific, and transparent.

Go all the way down to your control variables.

Assign people to the task and let them do their job.

On the road again.

If you want to get there, you gotta keep moving.

You have quite a journey ahead. I've already told what the three strategies are and how to use them. Now, let me give you the last piece of this puzzle: Getting everything together and start working on your customers' loyalty.

Let's make it a step by step guide, something like a recipe. If families keep traditions this way, I will borrow the idea to let this new business tradition be kept and spread –yes, I see it as a near future tradition.

Ready? Take note.

Recipe for a Customer Excellence Program.

You will need:

A leader.

A team of enthusiastic, persistent, objectives oriented people who love their customers: The *Customer Excellence Ambassadors*.

"The" operations guy.

"The" human resources guy.

Two information technology guys; one of them has to be familiar with databases, for both design and query.

Some process people.

One or two human resources people.

A "What we need to do" budget. You will use it over several years, so think a fourth of it per year.

A communications group –it can be internal or external. If external, add around $7,500 per month for professional fees. This group is comprised of a planner, a creative copywriter, an account executive and a production executive. Graphic design, industrial design and other support roles may be of use on certain occasions.

A spokesperson.

An action plan.

Lots of enthusiasm.

Be sure you find two qualities on any people you choose to get your list complete: Enthusiasm and customer orientation. You don't want to spoil your recipe because you got a guy who thinks customers are a pain in the butt, and brings no positive attitude to the table.

To prepare your team, think about two to three months. First of all, start by getting your strategic plan in place and communicate it to the whole organization. If you want this recipe to go right, you need everybody in, or at least aware, about the loop.

Put your vision together and set a date for it. A normal time is three years. Write it down, and follow the traditional strategic planning process: From goals to strategies, to tactics... and publish it. Get the graphic designer and copywriter from your team, and make them turn your ideas and plan into a nice, appealing one-piecer, so simple and easy to read that everybody in the organization is capable of understanding it. And I mean everybody, in every office, in every position, has to understand it. Forget about business jargon, complicated ideas, go for easy pieces –meme-like style– and send it out.

At the same time, do some analysis. Find out the customers which have the higher impact on your revenue and profits. Paretto comes quite handy here; look for the biggest part of your profits, and find which customers generate them –like in a traditional 80-20 analysis, even when you may well find a different ratio; don't worry, play it as it comes.

Study your valuable customers. Call their account managers and ask for details, their story, their anecdotes, and write everything now. After this, they will be the heroes, the stars, the untouchables, and the organization will get to know who they are, why they are important, and to treat them with total care. These customers, your *Red Phone* customers, will be the foundation for your success.

Now, when you know who your *Red Phones* are, send the communications out. If you need to send long, or several different messages, remember the rule: "One piece, one message". It means you will send one message per piece and, if needed, will design a second piece for the second and successive messages.

When writing the messages, think as if you were speaking with 12 year olds. Use simple, short words, on simple phrases. Proofread your messages and, if needed, go to one of your lower education peers and ask them to explain the content back to you. If they can't explain the message to you, redo your piece. Remember: You are not writing to win a prize; your customers must understand your message without any doubts.

Once your piece is ready, send it out. Publish it. Use your main communications media, and give it eight columns, the front page, the biggest font. Present it as the most important news of this year. Why? Because you need people to understand that your company is focusing on get-and-keep loyal customers, and they are the foundation of a healthy company, with healthy results… which is good for everybody, from owners and investors, to the lowest ranked employee.

Once the piece is published, your public relations work begins. Yes, you embarked on a long journey, and it will ask for unusual activities from you. Maybe you are the CEO, or the CMO, or the COO, and maybe you've never had to spread your enthusiasm about anything; however, things are different. You assigned yourself the most important and relevant task of your company: keeping a profitable and beneficial relationship with your customers –with benefits for both sides, to get everybody something good.

Gather small groups; up to 15 people will be enough. Have breakfast with them; have lunch with them; have walks with them. Look for any way to get their undivided attention and trust while you are telling them two things: What the company will do, and how you plan on doing it.

Yes. This is when you talk about the three strategies, and break them down into the three major tactics you will put in place: First, the Customer Excellence Ambassadors; second, the Red Phone customers; third, your vision on how to keep and grow your business with them –and this is the most important part; This is where you talk about the Three Laws of Customer Conservation; this is where you will either get or lose your people's enthusiasm.

To be convincing, remember this formula: Say what you will do, say why you will do it, say how are you going to do it. In that order. It works.

> *Say why you will do it,*
> *say what you will do,*
> *say how are you going to do it.*

As in old fashion learning instructions: repeat, then repeat, then repeat, as much as needed. You have to get fans for your movement. If you only have people who are interested, nothing will happen. You need people who are willing to do things, to change the status quo, to take their company's relationships with customers to a new height. So, repeat, and repeat, and repeat. If you may publish again a new version of your piece, do it. Get people from the C suite to talk about your initiative and how beneficial it will be for the company and its customers. Get them to be your advocates, and a heavy weight will get off your shoulders: and get them to tell the right message. Be relentless on what and how it will happen, and get them to learn it. You own the plan, they are facilitators.

After one or two months, everybody will have at least read about the new Customer Excellence Program. Now, it is time for stage two: Implementation.

According to my experience, two to three months after they are delivered to people, messages are forgotten and initiatives die. You have less than three months after you give your message to start walking the talk. So, pick the date to have the first formal activity with one or some of your *Red Phone* customers, and go for it.

Gather your communications team and prepare something to let those customers know how special they are. For instance, think about a video, where you make the CEO explain, in the most personal manner, what the company will do for them: Improved response time, revised and improved quality assurance procedures, new rights or exclusive operating conditions they will get because of their importance… and be sure both operations and human resources guys know about those actions and are ready to deliver them with their teams. If they are not, everything will go down the drain, and you just don't want it to happen.

Improved response time requires some new rules. *"Red Phone customers will have immediate response, meaning all their requests will be solved before 24 hours"* or *"The Customer Service office has the authority to overrule any decision on response times or people assignment, when it comes to solve a request from a Red Phone customer"*.

It also requires empowerment. To enforce those rules, you need to give power to your people. Everybody who is devoted to attending a *Red Phone* will have enough power as to authorize things way above their formal position, so they have to be customer oriented and equipped with the metrics and tools to know three things: How many requests are they solving per period, how satisfied their customers are, and what decisions they made to achieve that.

The purpose is simple: If you can measure it, you can manage.

If you can measure it, you can manage it.

Once you start sending this message to your customers, be sure to plan a regular flow of communications towards them, and the corresponding channel to get their answers. A simple way to do it is divide your customers in three big segments, *Red Phone*, *Important*, and *Regular*.

Regular customers are those who purchase from you in normal conditions, pay normal amounts of money, and expect regular service. They may (yes, may) even have a positive attitude towards your company and products, even though they may be customers of other vendors at the same time, "just to be safe". Treat them in accordance to your quality standards, procedures and regular response times. Be sure you set the highest level of service possible –that's where your Chief Operations Officer comes very handy– and make them receive what they purchased, what they expect, when you agreed to deliver.

See? It is simple. Let's continue.

Important customers are similar to *Regulars*, with an exception: They purchase from you in <u>above</u> normal conditions, pay normal or above normal amounts of money, and expect better than regular service. They may (yes, may) even have a positive attitude towards your company and products, even though they may purchase from other vendors at the same time, "not putting all our eggs in a single basket". They have other business opportunities you may serve, and that's why they are interesting. You can make more money from them, giving them additional value.

Red Phone customers are the most valuable. They prefer your company, have been with it for years, resist your competitors' efforts to take them away, and even have a positive attitude towards your people, products and services. Dealing with them, there's just one rule that applies: All procedures, policies, customs and traditions will be bended when it comes to serving them, to satisfy their requests. Their needs are notified to the appropriate levels to approve exceptions and get authorizations and solve their problems... with one exception to the rule: No flexibility on ethics nor safety (I think you understand why).

There's a fourth segment I seldom speak about. They are the *Unknowns*. Customers whose value is unknown or negative; whose loyalty is unknown; who have an unknown potential. Unless you have a plan to do something with them, just keep in mind the Second Law of Customer Conservation –Each and every customer get what your business model promises, with no excuses– and move on.

See? Those segments are simple to define and manageable. Your COO, your CFO, they have to be aware of that, so the operations team may define the policies and procedures to treat those customers according to the value they represent to the company, the value they expect from the company, and their specific needs, with the financial people having their backs. It's an easy approach, and grading customers according to it will let you treat them as they deserve.

If they only get value from you, they are *Regular*. If they also give you value, they are *Important*. If they give you much value, you are of much value to them, and they share their specific needs to help you solve them, they are *Red Phone* customers. If there's nothing important to say or think about them, they are *Unknowns*.

Easy peasy, lemon squeezy.

Divide your customers into three groups, and revise them every quarter. The *Red Phones* have to be a few, a handful. You can't have many of them. As a rule, they have to be less than 1% of your total customers. *Important* customers may be up to 15%. The rest are *Regulars* and *Unknowns*.

Why these percentages? Because you want *Red Phones* to be the tip of the pyramid. They have to know they belong to an exclusive group, and you can even call your group that way: One percent. Just imagine the impact on an important customer telling them they are *One Percent*. The *Important* group is a runner-up contest. You can even tell them what do they need to become *One Percent*, and they will go for it, you bet. I've seen it. I've even seen one customer, who was ranked as number four, ask the company's CEO what to do to become number one. If it happens to you, ask for specific things, such as the product lines or amounts they need to purchase, terms and conditions, bonuses or discount policies –yes, when it comes to ego, this negotiation works like a charm.

Now, with all the ingredients ready, you are all set to go. Remember, this is a recipe, and you as the chef may use the ingredients in the manner you find best.

For instance, IT guys. They will come handy for activities such as getting the data to calculate which customers come into what group. Your spokesperson will see action when you talk to your employees or your customers, and a master of ceremony/speaker is needed to give formality, like those times when somebody trustable has to send a message throughout all your organization. The spokesperson will be sending the message, so you better make sure this person is fluent, understands customers and business, and has a way with people… you don't want your message lost because the messenger picked a fight with one attendee.

What about Human Resources areas? Well, they are your salt. You will need them, regardless of which actions you take. When training customer service people, or technicians, or any other employees, wether they face the customer or not, HR is always the best ally to overcome barriers, get the message through, and get people to act at unison towards a common goal. Like with the other guys on the recipe, look for HR people who likes and understand customers and their impact on the company. It'll be a plus for their performance.

TAKE AWAYS

Get the right people from different areas and let everybody know what's it all about –including customers.

Segment customers, and treat them in accordance.

Align policies and procedures with customer segments.

Spread the word and adjust your policies and procedures to accommodate your words.

Ready, set, swim!

Sometimes, the only option is to jump into the pool.

I developed the three strategies to solve a challenge: How to use an academic finding in the real business world. What was known as the COS Model in my doctoral thesis, turned into three strategies, and they proved to be successful in the business world, too.

I just gave you my best advice on how to implement them, and lead your organization to the world of loyal customers, with all its perks and benefits.

This book was intended as a piece of advice for managers out there who are sick and tired of loosing customers, trying to do something useful while the rest of the world is whining *"Poor me, customer loyalty is dead, oh, poor me!"*

Now, let me give you my final advice: Trust your guts and follow your best judgement.

This is the management world. There's no truth written on stone. I will give you my manifesto on how to manage, so you can make the necessary decisions when embarking on this journey to managing your customers' loyalty and increase three variables: Customer retention, average sales per customer, and customer satisfaction.

My Customer Manifesto.

Customers are the most important thing for us. Nothing else, nobody else can compete with them. We live because of them. Our income comes from them. Customers defeat everything else.

We make things happen. On time. As promised. No buts nor ifs. We assume our responsibility.

Our execution is impeccable. We don't leave at random what we can control. We act orderly, making sure to go towards the results our customers expect. Our communications with customers, vendors and allies are frank and constant. We make sure we make things happen.

We look for demanding, first class customers, who are focused on reaching their goals. Visionaries. Challenging customers. Customers who are eager to win, to grow, to be better. A good customer makes us become a better version of ourselves. A good customer is the best thing that can happen to us.

Talented, intelligent people, who are good at work, respected and happy, are people with whom it is a pleasure to work with. Listening to their thoughts, understanding their points of view, collaborating and co-creating with them is a privilege.

Resources must be enough to get results, never excessive. Excess on resources creates a sensation of being already there, of conformity with the task at hand... both attitudes conflict with the desire to win.

Austerity is a good way to live and work. We humans are where we are because of our need to fight with limited resources. It spurs ingenuity and stimulates us to create.

Those who work for us have to be better prepared, smarter, more capable than us. When having people like this, we run a team of giants, unstoppable; a winner.

Nobody is essential. Beginning with me.

Business continuity is my responsibility. Keeping customers is my responsibility. My team is my responsibility.

Work is a passion. Passions are to be loved. If I don't love my work, I must leave it.

My family is my identity and core to my happiness. It is a part of me, and I have it with me when I'm working. My family is my motivation. I share my wins with them. If my family is not a part of me, something is very wrong.

If there's conflict between my family and my job, it is my obligation to resolve it. None of them can suffer for my inability to make decisions.

Balance between say and do is fundamental. If I say more than I do, it is bad. I am a liar. If I do more than I say, it is also bad. I'm a micromanager. What I say has to be equal to what I do. It provides balance.

Loyalty to my staff is paramount. They are my team. They depend on me. I get results because of them, they must know they may count on me.

Loyalty to my company is essential to be successful. It shows. Customers like it and competitors are challenged by it.

Loyalty to my customers is an immovable rule. I purchase their products, I use their services. Those actions show I believe in them as they believe in me and my work. I try hard to understand their business, their challenges and problems. I look for their success before mine.

Competition can be my friend and I respect it, even though I know we are after each other's customers, without mercy. Competing according to the rules of chivalry, I will shoot to kill when needed.

Environment is not an accessory. It is my world. I respect it and look after it. When my decisions have something to do with it, I take it very seriously.

Ethics do matter. Ethical behavior is my responsibility, both from me and my team's side. When I run over somebody else with my decisions and do them wrong, I have to review my ethical sense.

Life is one and it is worth living it right. To have fun, to rest, to learn. We are here to believe, to create, to wait.

TAKE AWAYS

You are the manager.

You lead, you make the calls.

Your results and your team's are your responsibility.

So, what do you think now? Is customer loyalty dead, or alive & well?

I did look at fear right in the eye.
Fear got afraid and left.

Thanks, Grandpa!

© Lalo Duron, PhD, 2019.

All rights reserved.

This book became a reality thanks to my editor, Annie Duron, who is my daughter and business partner.

The Hartman Institute. Canada and Mexico.